Entrepreneur® MENTOR SERIES

W9-AGG-055

SUCCESSFUL BUSINESS MODELS

Surefire Ways to Build a Profitable Business

DON DEBELAK

EP
Entrepreneur® Press

Editorial Director: Jere Calmes
Cover Design: Beth Hanson-Winter
Composition: CWL Publishing Enterprises, Inc., Madison, WI,
www.cwlpub.com

This publication is designed to provide accurate and authorita-
tive information in regard to the subject matter covered. It is sold
with the understanding that the publisher is not engaged in ren-
dering legal, accounting, or other professional services. If legal
advice or other expert assistance is required, the services of a
competent professional person should be sought.
—From a Declaration of Principles jointly adopted by a
Committee of the American Bar Association and
a Committee of Publishers and Associations

ISBN 1-891984-45-4

Printed in Canada

09 08 07 06 05   10 9 8 7 6 5 4 3 2

CONTENTS

PREFACE

Over the last 15 years, I've worked with dozens of new businesses, putting together plans and strategies and doing feasibility analyses of their proposed ventures. I've become increasingly aware over the years that people like to follow the business plan format, starting with an executive summary and covering all aspects of the business from management to production, without really evaluating the feasibility of their concept.

As I write this book in the fall of 2001 and spring of 2002, it has become obvious that most dot-coms have failed and that many new business approaches that came to the fore in the late 1990s and early 2000s didn't really work, despite their great business plans and substantial investment.

The companies that did succeed followed, either on purpose or by accident, most of the business concepts that I've found over the last 15 years influenced the success of any new business. The core of those principles is what I refer to as the GEL factors, **G**reat customers, **E**asy sales, and **L**ong life—the factors that in effect gel business ideas into profitable businesses.

The dot-com collapse did something else that really led me to write this book. It collapsed the myth that the business plan was what really counts for business success. What has become obvious to many entrepreneurs is that businesses need to concentrate first on creating a winning business concept and then, second, on turning that concept into a forward-thinking business plan.

The Format

The book is divided into two sections: the first on what I call the *GEL factors analysis*, a method of evaluating your business concept and then determining how it can be improved for a better chance of success; the second on how to write a business plan that will really sizzle.

The first section is divided into two parts. The first explains the GEL factors for success and includes a chapter of checklists at the end that will help you evaluate the GEL factors for your business concept. The second part of the section is GEL factor analyses of a variety of businesses. These case studies will help you better understand how a GEL factor analysis works.

In the business plan section of the book, I've included three business plans. One plan is used throughout the business plan chapters to show how the advice in those sections can be implemented. The last two plans are samples of how plans are written when entrepreneurs are seeking an investment. These plans are not overly long, but give a succinct look at each company's philosophy, business model, and implementation plan.

Writing the Plan

I've written dozens of business plans. Great plans always start with an analysis of your business. The reason you write a plan is that it forces you to revaluate your business. When people tell me that they haven't written a plan for three or four years, they usually justify it based on the fact that their business hasn't changed. I believe that what they are telling me is that, in fact, they are flying by the seat of the pants. Everyone's business changes every year, and often every six months. Customers, competition, and distribution are all changing and an entrepreneur who doesn't reevaluate his or her business is taking a real chance. Entrepreneurs should do a plan every year—if for no other reason than the fact that businesses make big money when they are first to uncover a new market need.

Tips and Stories

Throughout the book you'll find four boxes, each offering different types of information:

1. *Definitions of words and jargon:* Concepts that are frequently used in venture capital and entrepreneur circles but that are not always well known by small business owners.

2. *Company stories:* Each chapter in the business model section includes a story about a company that used the tactic highlighted in the chapter. These stories should help you see that average companies are transforming their businesses every year. Plus, I hope the stories give you a better understanding of how companies have used their creativity to find a wide variety of strategies to make their businesses successful.

3. *Insights:* Some sidebar boxes give you answers to the questions business owners commonly ask me, such as "How do I set my price?" or "How much money will I need to introduce a product or service?"

4. *GEL Factor Medallions.* These are listed next to every story about a company and will rate the business being discussed. It will have a "yes" or "no"

> **G = Yes**
> **E = Yes**
> **L = No**

listed after each of the three letters G, E, and L. A "yes" means the company does have Great customers, Easy sales, or Long life, while a "no" means it doesn't. The medallions are to help you start to analyze companies by these three critical factors.

My goal in writing this book is threefold. First, I want to give you a new way to look at your business idea or your current business to find different strategies that could dramatically improve your sales and profits. Second, I want to help you realize how a business plan can be more than just a tool for raising money or for creating a budgeting process, how it can instead be a tool that reevaluates and strategically positions your business every year. Third, I want to offer you new skills for managing your strategic planning process.

Good luck and, most of all, good planning! I encourage you not to rush through the book, but to take the time to formulate your own winning model and plan as you read the book. Your future depends on it.

Don Debelak
DSD Marketing
P.O. Box 120861
New Brighton, MN 55112

Acknowledgments

For providing the business plan Princeton WebSolutions: The National Foundation for Teaching Entrepreneurship (NFTE), New York, New York.

For providing most of the information on the financial section of the business plan: Jim Lewin, BizPlanIt, Scottsdale, Arizona.

For providing the business plan for SanaSana: M. Elizabeth Barton, Carlos R. DeJesus, Adam W. Farkas, M.D., and Ricardo Fernandez, alumni of the University of Michigan MBA program.

For providing the business plan for The Boulder Shop: Luke Walsh, Owner of The Boulder Shop in Boulder, Colorado, and Doug Wilson, Palo Alto Software in Eugene, Oregon.

I also want to thank Jere Calmes, editorial director at Entrepreneur Press, for his support during the writing of this book and John Woods and the team at CWL Publishing Enterprises for their help in putting the final product together.

SECTION I
PART ONE

▲ ▲ ▲

THE GEL
FACTORS
HOW TO EVALUATE
YOUR BUSINESS

THE GEL FACTORS: PREDICTING SUCCESS

SUCCESS: EASY AND COMPLICATED

T he last 10 years have been a wild ride for new business ventures, from the dot-com to the dot-bomb era. During this explosive heyday, everyone involved felt invincible, unable to fail. The acronyms and buzzwords flew, the world was full of pumped-out chests and fabulous fortunes, and no one could do any wrong.

How wrong they turned out to be! Business fundamentals never stopped counting and the companies that had the right customers, the right product, and the right business concept succeeded.

The GEL Factors

The three main characteristics for predicting success are what I refer to as the GEL Factors for success:

1. They have **G**reat customers.
2. Sales are relatively **E**asy to make.
3. The business will have a **L**ong life.

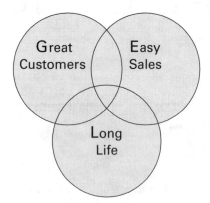

FIGURE 1-1. GEL: Overlapping factors in success

A business will make a lot of money for a long time if it possesses all three GEL factors. To determine whether or not a business has these three points, you need to evaluate customers, products, distribution networks, technical support, new product development, and production.

Pitfalls to Avoid

At the peak of the dot-com era, investors and entrepreneurs became infatuated with the term business model. Models had to do with how a business operated and had little to do with customers, how easy sales would be, or how sustainable a business might be. Avoid basing your business on another company's business model until you can be sure all the GEL (**G**reat Customers, **E**asy Sales, **L**ong Life) factors for success are present.

The GEL factor evaluation isn't a pass-fail test; it's to determine what's wrong with your business approach so that you can repair it. Once you're able to fine-tune your business so it delivers all GEL factors, you'll be able to write a great business plan.

How will you know if your business has these success points? That's what this first section of the book is all about—dissecting your business so you know you have great customers, easy sales, and a long life. In reality, most new businesses won't have all the success elements in place at first. That's not a problem. This section of the book will show you how to modify your business operation so it will really sizzle. Figure 1-2 details the evaluation points of your GEL factor evaluation.

GREAT CUSTOMERS	Characteristics	Number Ease of Finding Spending Patterns
	Value to You	$ Value of Sale Repeat Sales Ongoing Sales Support
EASY SALES	Value to Customer	How Important Competitive Advantage Price/Value Relationship
	Customer Acquisition Cost	Entry Points Sales Support Required Promotional Activities
LONG LIFE	Profit per Sale	Margins Up-Selling and Cross-Selling Selling Cost per Sale
	Investment Required	To Enter Business To Keep Market Share To Stay on the Cutting Edge

FIGURE 1-2. GEL factors for a successful business

Starbucks—Brewing Success One Cup at a Time

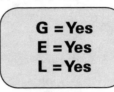

G = Yes
E = Yes
L = Yes

Starbucks is a great example of a company with all the success points. Its great customers are upper-income people who like to pamper themselves. There are a large number of those customers: they are easy to find by their neighborhoods and where they work, and they spend freely. Those customers provide plenty of value to the company because the dollar value of their sale is much higher than at traditional coffee shops, repeat business is great (like two to five times a week), and the ongoing product support costs are very low as people consume the product.

Starbucks also scores high on the easy sales criterion, starting with its value to the customers. The Starbucks "premium quality" image is important to its customers, its products are better than coffee from a coffee cart or a fast-food restaurant, and its prices, though higher than its competitors', are still a bargain for the image they create for the consumer. In terms of acquiring customers, Starbucks started in Seattle, where it could afford the number of stores and promotion it needed and its name recognition means minimal ongoing support.

As for long life, Starbucks meets all the profitability tests and its ongoing support is minimal once it has established its brand. There were only two questions when looking at the Starbucks concept before it opened its first store: first, whether or not its target customers would feel premium brands of coffee and bakery items make them feel good about themselves and second, how often customers would come back to Starbucks. Both of those questions could be answered at the test store that Starbucks opened in the Seattle market.

Kinko's—Tweaking the Concept

G = No
E = No
L = Yes

Kinko's started out as a copy center at major colleges and universities. To create recurring revenue, it offered students copies of articles or papers that professors wanted to distribute for their classes. Kinko's would get a list of desired handouts from professors, then arrange for the rights to copy them and sell them to students. The idea behind the concept was that Kinko's would have a lot of products to sell to a lot of students. As an additional service, Kinko's added computer work stations that students could use 24 hours a day.

This business approach had many elements for success. It provided a service that professors wanted, it offered easy access to thousands of customers (who also—Kinko's hoped—would make plenty of copies of other documents), and it produced a steady revenue stream.

There was just one problem: the work involved for each sale was just too high. Kinko's needed just too many employees to execute its strategy for the fees it collected, especially for the work required to make copies for one class. This could have been the end of the story—except that Kinko's strategy of being open 24 hours a day had a side benefit. Kinko's started getting jobs for overnight production of copies of documents for businesses. And not just small jobs: financial memorandums, presentations, court documents, and a whole range of other jobs for which businesses waited till the last minute to make copies.

So Kinko's switched its business approach. It started locating its stores near large business centers, where there were always lots of businesses that needed to make last minute copies. All of a sudden, Kinko's model changed, focusing on businesses instead of students. The old model had as its target customers students who watched their money closely. The new model had as its target customers companies that would pay almost anything to get the rush job they needed on time. Students thought a $20 purchase was big. Companies were happy spending hundreds and even thousands of dollars to get their documents on time.

The results are clear. The new approach has a much better group of customers, who were easy to identify and happy to spend money to meet their needs. The new customer group is all it took to turn Kinko's into a profitable powerhouse.

The Business Concept vs. the Business Plan

You can write a great business plan for a business approach that just doesn't work for your customers and products and you just won't make any money. A business plan is an indispensable tool for charting the course of your business. A great business idea will still fail if it doesn't have a strong business plan behind it.

But the fact is that the foundation for success is a sound business operation that has all three key success points of the GEL factors evaluation. Once you have the foundation, you will be ready to move on to the business plan. That's how you will make your plan sizzle.

FINDING A GREAT CUSTOMER GROUP

FIGURING OUT WHO VALUES WHAT YOU CAN OFFER

> **G**reat customers are probably the most important element for a highly profitable business. They allow companies to make strong profits and to enjoy steady sales increases. Great customers aren't necessarily the customers with the most money, but they're the customers who value what you offer and are willing to pay for it. More importantly, they're the customers who will keep buying from you repeatedly and their purchases are significant to your profits.
>
> I don't mean to imply by the title of the chapter that there's only one right group of customers. All customer groups buy many products and there is a different right customer group for every product. These may sound like some pretty stiff requirements, but in fact many businesses are able to attract and keep a great group of customers.

The Real Life Works Here but Not There

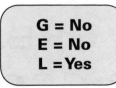

G = No
E = No
L = Yes

Rainforest Café had a brief run of success in the late '90s in both high-traffic vacation or destination sites and upscale neighborhoods. At first the restaurants were all a success. But after a few years, Rainforest closed its restaurants that weren't at travel destination spots. What happened?

Rainforest's target customer group is people who want to go to an upscale theme restaurant where the theme is more important than the food. At destinations, with a steady stream of new people, there were always enough customers. But away from destinations, people only occasionally wanted to visit a theme restaurant and there just weren't enough customers to keep buying its product.

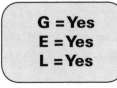

G = Yes
E = Yes
L = Yes

Buca is a theme restaurant chain that is growing fast around the country. It is a parody of Italian restaurants, with pictures all over the walls, little grotto scenes, and tons of Italian kitsch décor.

Why is Buca different? Its average price per dinner is $15 to $20 per person, including a drink or two. At that price, many people are not only willing to visit the restaurant, but ready to visit it regularly.

In contrast, Rainforest's bill typically runs over $30 per person. That upscale price lowered the number of potential customers to the point that there just weren't enough to support the business at locations away from travel destinations.

SIX KEY FACTORS FOR EVALUATING CUSTOMERS

		Desired	Excellent	Average	Poor
Customer Characteristics	Number	High			
	Ease of Finding	Easy			
	Spending Patterns	Prolific			
Customer Value to Company	$ Value of Sale	High			
	Repeat Sales	Many			
	Ongoing Sales Support	Low			

FIGURE 2-1. GEL factor customer checklist

Number

Why It's Important

Businesses have three problems when it comes to the number of potential customers. One is that they have a cost of doing business and that cost can only be overcome by doing business with enough customers to pay the bill. The second is that owners have income expectations that they need to meet. The third is that a business needs a certain momentum to succeed and it needs to promote itself. You might not have income to afford the promotion you need to attract customers if the number of potential prospects is too small.

When It's a Key Concern

1. *Your product or service is inexpensive.* A low-price product needs lots of customers to make money.
2. *Opportunities for repeat or add-on sales are limited.* If you need new customers every year, you need a big prospect pool.
3. *When customers can't find your business easily.*

Customers look for some businesses in the Yellow Pages. If they don't look for your type of business, then you have to find them.

4. *People don't know about your type of product, business, or service.* They won't be looking for you if they don't know you exist.

How to Compensate

1. *You can present a compelling reason to buy.* You can get by with fewer prospects if your concept significantly meets a major customer desire.
2. *You can have a devoted distribution channel.* For example, people who buy map-related products are a small, widely scattered group of customers go out of their way to find the few map stores that are in their area.
3. *You can be in places where your customers go.* A store that wants to sell ceramic tiles for home address numbers or garden plaques, for example, might thrive if located in a mall or town with a concentration of artisan stores and shops.
4. *You can be part of a network of organizations serving the same customer group.* You can promote effectively if you combine your efforts with other companies serving the market.

Ease of Finding

Why It's Important

You need to either easily locate customers or be easy for them to locate you. If it's hard to find customers, you may need to spend, spend, spend to find them and that cost might prohibit your success. For example, how does a company that sells small, in-home soda dispensers, similar to the ones in fast-food restaurants, find customers when only

*O*nce you tightly define your customer group, check to be sure that there are successful businesses that appear to be targeting the same customer group. List what is similar about what the companies are offering and what is different. Pay particular attention to the price, the amount of repeat business, and the importance of the product to the customer. Be wary of customer groups that don't support successful businesses.

a small number of people will want the hassles of an in-home carbonated soda machine? Who are they and how can you find them?

When It's a Key Concern

Anytime that you can't depend on the following means of finding customers easily:

1. *Customers belong to clubs or associations related to your product.*
2. *There are trade or consumer magazines targeted at your customer group.*
3. *Customers can be identified through purchased lists.*
4. *Big events or trade shows target your customer group.*
5. *A distribution market serves your market.* Special wood-working shops or wild bird catalogs, for example, are targeted at customers who would otherwise be hard to find.
6. *Customers know where to look for you.* For example, people looking to go hunting in Montana look for lodges on the Internet or in hunting magazines.

How to Compensate

1. *Consolidate several products or services into a high-dollar purchase that will justify spending lots of money to locate a few customers.*
2. *Find potential customers through current customers.* A painter specializing in high-appeal party rooms knows that one person who loves to entertain knows many others who like to do the same, which can lead to referral business.
3. *Create a joint marketing campaign with other companies serving the same target group facing the same problem of finding customers.*

*To be considered a **customer group**, people need to act in a similar manner. For example, people who cook dinner after eight hours of work are not a customer group. They'll behave differently depending on whether they have children, how many people they cook for, and whether or not they use prepared foods. A customer group would be working people who minimize their use of prepared food and are concerned about nutrition.*

4. *Offer classes or seminars or attend trade shows to attract prospects.* A company that offers services to convert lawns into natural wildlife gardens might offer classes and demonstrations or start a club for people interested in a yard with natural fauna.

Spending Patterns
Why It's Important

Some customer groups buy primarily on emotion and they will spend freely. Parents of young children may spend on impulse. Companies that want to be perceived as being leading-edge typically will spend money to protect their image. How customers spend impacts a company in two ways. The first is that customers who spend freely typically require less sales effort and customer service than customers who watch their money closely. The second is that customers who spend freely will often make bigger purchases, which simply results in more sales for less effort.

When It's a Key Concern

1. *The sale is based on practical considerations rather than an emotional response.* People will almost always spend freely when it's an emotional purchase, such as a car, but they're always looking to cut costs for practical purchases.
2. *The product is not a priority purchase for the customer.* Customers who are reluctant will still always buy if it's a high priority for them.
3. *You don't have the resources to provide an intensive sales effort.* You can't shortchange the sales effort unless the customer is spending freely.
4. *The product needs to be purchased only once.* Unless your product is consumed and frequently purchased, you

> *C*onfused customers never buy. Customers don't think the same way a salesperson does. Salespeople sell their product features, while customers worry about how a product will solve their problems or meet their desires. You'll always sell more if you gear your sales and marketing efforts toward showing the customers how they will meet their goals with your product.

can afford only a limited sales effort for each sale and a limited sales effort won't sell customers who watch every penny.

How to Compensate

1. *Find a way to translate your sale into an emotional purchase.* Subway did a great job with its promotion of the student who lost over 100 pounds eating low-fat Subway subs. Giving people an easy way to lose weight stirs up powerful emotions.

2. *Sell a complete solution.* Find out what the customers feel is their goal when they buy your products or services and add products or services to help the customers achieve their overall goal.

3. *Set sales policies to make the buying decision easy.* 30-day trials, guaranteed returns, leases, and monthly fees versus a straight purchase are all ways to make the purchase decision easier for the customer.

4. *Concentrate your efforts on big potential accounts.* Most salespeople will tell you it's just as much work to sell $5,000 to a small company as it is to sell $200,000 to a big company.

5. *Add a product or a service that your potential customer will look for.* For example, people don't know where to look for invention marketing services. A firm might add prototype services, which its customers do look for in their Yellow Pages.

Dollar Value of Sale
Why It's Important

A high-dollar sale automatically creates a high-value customer. That means that a company can afford to devote resources to the customer, knowing that the sale will result in a profit. A company that supplies fuel stations for compressed natural gas vehicles may have an average sale price of $750,000. It can afford the sales support the customer needs to make a buying decision. On the other hand, a $5,000 to $8,000 industrial sale, especially to a small business, can be a dangerous price point, because the price still requires extensive sales support, but the size of the sale doesn't produce the necessary profits.

> *W*hen you're having trouble locating customers, ask yourself what characteristics of customers make them strong candidates to buy your product. For the soda machine distributor, the people most likely to buy might be mid-to high-income people with more than three kids or people who have lots of kids around, like coaches. Those are people that the company could find and sell, so it would have a chance to succeed.

When It's a Key Concern

1. *Sales support is required.* Sales of complex or technical items require an extensive sales effort, as do sales that are important for a company's operation and sales for which the final buying decision involves many people.

2. *Products are customized for each customer.* A person installing rock gardens needs to plan, select the right materials, and offer plenty of hand-holding support.

3. *The sales cycle is long.* Most families spend a lot of time thinking and planning before deciding to go ahead with a major home redecorating project. Many business-to-business sales start with an assessment of the available products, a preliminary request for budget approval, and then a final analysis by many people before a product is purchased.

4. *There are many competitors.* Your closing rate will typically be lower if you have many competitors, which means that you will have to make a large number of sales calls for every order you receive.

5. *There are few opportunities for follow-up sales.* People put up vinyl siding only once in the time they own a home. They might, in contrast, buy a new entertainment system every three to four years.

How to Compensate

1. *Sell a turnkey solution.* A product that is integrated into a system requires a great sales effort, because the customer has a lot to worry about: in the end he or she is responsible for making sure the system works.

2. *Get the customers to come to you.* An average sales call can cost a company anywhere from $200 to $800. You can minimize that cost by having customers come to your location. Demonstrations, trainings, special events, and plant tours are all ways to attract customers to your location.

3. *Create an independent sales network.* Independent sales agents receive a commission on what they sell. Typically, companies have only minimal upfront fees with sales agents.

4. *Add product lines.* One way to increase the dollar value of each sale is to add complementary products so you have more items to sell. You can add your own new products or start to sell products from other companies.

> **Closing rate** is a term that states the percentage of prospects who give you an order. A 5% closing rate means that 5% of the prospects buy. Try to determine which type of prospects has the best closing rate for you and then concentrate on them.

Repeat Sales

Why It's Important

Regular repeat sales are where companies can find really big profits. The sales costs are low, product support costs are usually low, and typically customers buy a standard product for which manufacturing costs are low. Companies can spend lots of money to get customers who will buy repeatedly and they can spend money to develop a strong relationship with those customers.

The Market Niche

For the last 20 years, marketing has been about the *market niche* or, as the venture capitalists call it today, the space a company operates in. I don't mean to suggest in this chapter that the focus on a market segment or customer group (otherwise known as a *niche*) is not important. The goal of a business is to provide value to a customer; it can do that best by focusing on one group. You'll have a much easier time making money if you have a lot of free spending, easy-to-find customers than if you try scratching out a living from a few, hard-to-find, tightwad customers. That's the point of the GEL analysis, finding a way to operate that will make it easy to make money.

When It's a Key Concern

1. *The dollar value of each sale is small.* It's difficult to drive down the cost of sales. It costs money to create a customer file, check credit, and monitor results even if a customer just calls you out of the blue to order.

2. *Customer service costs are high.* Selling to large customers, selling a product that interfaces with many other products, and selling a product with a large number of variations all typically require extensive customer service support.

3. *The purchase is a low-priority decision for customers.* It's difficult to get customers to make a purchase decision that they feel is a low priority. But it can still be worth the trouble to get the sale if it's an item people purchase regularly, such as office supplies, maintenance supplies, or telephone service.

4. *You have a small sales staff.* Customers making a major one-time purchase will be wary of a small company, because they will worry about after sales service. But they will be happy to buy from a smaller supplier items they purchase regularly.

How to Compensate

1. *Create a more important purchase decision.* Ask how you can turn your purchase into one that will have a meaningful impact on a customer. For example, painters who create a memorable faux finishing look for a home will obtain much more business than a painter offering a straight paint job.

2. *Find complementary ways to add value.* For the most part, what customers want is "no worries." Try to figure out what concerns a customer has about your type of purchase and then add services that make the decision "hassle-free."

3. *Create a low-cost sales plan.* You can keep sales costs low by selling on the Internet, through catalogs, through distributors and manufacturer's sales agents, at trade shows, or through another company.

4. *Expand the target market to a larger area.* If you can't get enough repeat business from your current market, you might need to expand to a bigger market. The bigger your target market, the more likely you'll find more customers eager to buy and your sales costs will be lower.

5. *Focus on big buyers.* Every market has big buyers, customers whose sales volume might justify your sales costs. If they don't, you need to reevaluate your business model.

Ongoing Sales Support

Why It's Important

When you sell office supplies, you don't need to offer much ongoing product support, which means that you get to keep most or all of the profit from each sale. But if you offer a lawn service that fertilizes lawns, you'll need more sup-

Controlling sales and marketing is a key to a successful business model. If you sell through distributors, sales and marketing costs—which include advertising, trade shows, direct mail, and brochures—should be no more than 20% to 22% of your sales revenue. If you sell direct to consumers, keep your costs below 30%.

port. People will call up and check on whether or not a treatment is safe for a pet or ask what to do if it rains right after the lawn is fertilized. All of these services cost money, and sometimes support costs can eliminate all the profits from a sale. Customers can represent high value to the company when they require little or no support, even if the profit margin per sale is low. The reverse is also true. An apparently profitable customer can quickly become a profit drain if support costs are high.

When It's a Key Concern

1. *Customers are buying an expected result instead of a defined product or service.* When people buy a food processor, for example, it's because they expect it will prepare some great exotic meals. Customers will complain if those meals don't come, even if the food processor works perfectly.
2. *Customer satisfaction depends on the application.* This is a common problem in business-to-business markets where customers have different applications. Some of those applications are bound to not work as well as others and that will create follow-up costs.
3. *The product is new and users aren't familiar with its operation.* People will typically have trouble with any new

Direct Costs

Most new companies badly underestimate the follow-up support required for products and services. Manufacturers find that people don't understand the simplest instructions and that they break products despite clear warnings. Service providers find that customers change their minds about what they want or ask for one change after another. Find out what your product support costs will be from someone already in the industry.

device. With established products, customers will accept problems with comments of "That's just the way a product works" or they'll be able to find someone who can help them use it.

4. *Products are customized to a customer's application.* You're offering a beta unit when you're selling a customized product or service. Beta units have tons of kinks that can be worked out only in the field, which requires tons of product support.

5. *Products interface with a number of other products.* Computer hardware and software products have only now, after two decades, started to interrelate well with each other and those interface problems created product support costs.

How to Compensate

1. *Design products so that use is intuitive and "idiot-proof."* Do you read manuals? Probably not. You expect products to be intuitive. Most people wait until a problem develops—and then call technical assistance.

2. *Manage customers' expectations.* To a large degree, the supplier sets customers' expectations. If your advertising, sales presentations, and brochures all promise the world's greatest product, that's what customers will expect.

3. *Choose your customers carefully.* Some customers have expectations you can't meet. Others have applications where your performance is marginal. Still others require ongoing support you can't afford.

4. *Offer training programs at your location.* Bringing the customers to your location is proactive, offers value to your customers, and is cost-effective for you.

> *Beta sites, beta units, and beta customers* are terms you hear all the time with new companies or products. They simply mean test sites or test units. Companies often put products and services out at beta sites for six to 12 months to make sure the products or services work. It's not uncommon for support on beta units to exceed 25% of the sales price.

*T*o determine just what expectations your customers have, ask your last 15 customers why they decided to buy from you, and what their expectations were. If those expectations are overly high, you have a major problem to correct. This is especially important for service providers, because customers can't see or touch what you're offering before buying.

5. *Sell through a network that can provide service.* Many industries—including power tools, lawn equipment, motorcycles, and industrial compressors—sell through a network of dealers that provide the service customers need.

Company Vignettes

Note to readers: I'll be tracking three companies—Dr. Spock Co., O'Naturals, and Jawroski's Towing and Service—throughout the first three chapters of this book to see how they compare on each GEL factor. The one point to notice is that a business needs all of the GEL factors for success.

There are six comparison factors:

1. Number of customers
2. Ease of finding
3. Spending patterns
4. Dollar value per sale
5. Potential for repeat sales
6. Ongoing sales support required

Dr. Spock Co.

Dr. Spock Co. provides parents advice on child rearing based upon the works of Dr. Spock.

Parents of babies, especially parents who are professionals and in their 30s, appeared to the founders to be the right customer group. Their goal is to become the number-one spot that parents come for baby advice, relying on the company's books, Web sites, and pamphlets.

Evaluation on the basis of customers:

1. Customers are older parents (28 years old and up); they are numerous. Score: +.
2. They are easy to locate through birth records, par-

enting shows, parenting magazine subscriptions, and purchases at child-oriented stores. Score: +.

3. This customer group is willing to spend money, and probably lots of money, for their children. It is not clear that customers value the advice of someone whose popularity peak was over 25 years ago (Dr. Spock). Score: Even.

4. The dollar value of each sale will be modest, probably $10 to $50, so the company may lose money on the first sale. Score: -.

5. Repeat sales could be strong, as children have new challenges as they grow older. Babies also go through stages very quickly, making it reasonable that customers will order every few months. Score: +.

6. The cost of ongoing customer support will be low. Information doesn't require warranty work or follow-up calls to be sure everything is working well. Score: +.

O'Naturals

O'Naturals is a chain of fast-food restaurants in New England that serve natural, organic foods.

Does fast food have to mean *fat* food? Not at O'Naturals, which is looking to gain a small part of the $20 billion natural food market. Its target customers are in wealthy New England towns that are populated by busy, highly educated, upper-income families.

Evaluation on the basis of customers:

1. Although the market for natural foods is large, the number of customers interested in a natural/organic restaurant is unclear, even in the carefully

chosen market. Score: Even.

2. People preferring natural organic food should be relatively easy to find through their interest in food coops, subscriptions in organic food magazines, and their trips to farmers' markets and other health food-oriented businesses. Score: +.

3. The target customers appear to be committed to health foods and they spend extra money for their food of choice. But they are also probably willing to take extra time to prepare food themselves. Score: Even.

4. The dollar sale value and profit per sale are modest, with a sale value of less than $7 per meal. Score: -.

5. The number of repeat sales should be high, since O'Naturals is one of only a few natural-food restaurants and the only fast-food option for most of its customers. If the customers like the food, they should keep coming back. Score: +.

6. The ongoing customer support element of a restaurant is average. There's no sales follow-up required, but O'Naturals must ensure a pleasant dining experience, from good service to a clean restaurant, to keep customers happy. Score: Even.

Jawroski's Towing and Service

Jawroski's is a car repair and towing business in a fast-growing suburban area.

This business generates 25% of its revenue from towing, 40% from fleet repairs, and 35% from consumer drive-in traffic. The business does about $1.3 million per year in revenue and has been growing at

25% a year with the growth of neighborhoods and businesses in the area. Most of Jawroski's towing business comes from vehicles that have broken down on a major freeway nearby.

Evaluation on the basis of customers:

1. Almost everyone over the age of 18 has at least one car and many businesses have sizeable fleets. Score: +.

2. Customers couldn't be easier to locate. People who need a tow go looking for a business to help them, the businesses with vehicle fleets can be found easily through county and state business records, and almost every home has a car. Score: +.

3. People need their cars and they will pay to have them towed and repaired. They may not always appreciate their car repair services, but they definitely have to purchase the service when their vehicle needs it. Score: +.

4. Car repairs rarely run under $100 and towing costs of $75 to $100 are common. These are substantial sales, which means the company needs only a small number of sales each day. Score: +.

5. Repeat sales should be good if Jawroski's delivers quality service. Many people go out of their way to a car repair shop where they've always gotten good service. Score: +.

6. Car repair shops don't have to work that hard to retain customers because people are leery of new shops. Car repair shops will keep their business as long as the shops give good service and keep current with technology changes. Score: +.

Many Ways to Skin a Cat

You've got stiff competition? Lucky for you there are still many methods you can use to build up a steady stream of business. I've listed here just a few of the tactics you can use.

1. *Make part of your business a consumable product that clients have to buy repeatedly.* Salt for water softeners, printer cartridges, and water for office coolers are all strong, consumable products.

2. *Provide ongoing service.* A lawn sprinkler system needs to be serviced in both spring and fall. Equipment suppliers to businesses frequently provide service contracts, both to produce ongoing revenue and to have the best chance of acquiring future business.

3. *Sell a service rather than a product.* Application service providers (ASPs) provide a server-to-host software for its customers for a monthly fee, rather than selling software.

4. *Spread your cost on a monthly basis, rather than requiring a major purchase—leases, service contracts, maintenance agreements that even costs out over time.* Customers are less likely to look for a new supplier if payments are low.

5. *Provide incentives for increased usage.* Airlines do this with frequent flyer miles, as do grocery stores that give customers extra incentives when they reach certain purchasing milestones. For companies selling consumable industrial products, a popular tactic is to increase discounts for ongoing purchases.

6. *Provide guaranteed trade-in value for upgrades.* Allow companies to upgrade your products for a fee and give you a trade-in for current products. This is especially effective in software and fast-changing technologies.

MAKING THE EASY SALE

MAKE SUCCESS HAPPEN ◀

For almost every thing they buy, your customers can choose from many products or services. Entrepreneurs understand this and realize that they have to have better value than their competition. But another fact often overlooked is that prospects buy only a small percentage of the products they could buy. You need to do more than just deliver better value than your competitors; you need to deliver better value than other companies supplying radically different products.

For example, an average worker looking for a way to relax might enjoy golf, fishing, boating, camping, resort vacations, hunting, or gambling. People don't have time to pursue all these activities and, to a large degree, the value they perceive for each activity will determine where they spend their money.

Entrepreneurs have two problems to overcome if they want truly easy sales. First, they need to offer something that customers really want to select among literally thousands of choices. Two, they need a cost-effective method of finding those customers and communicating with them.

Only One Winning Choice?

The battle is on for college students. Two new services are trying to appeal to college students looking for research to write that one great term paper. Questia has 50,000 primary textbooks and 4,000 journal articles online and charges $19.95 a month or $109.95 per year. Ebrary has over 17,000 books on line and searches are free, but copying documents costs from 15 to 25 cents per page. This is clearly a service college students want and will seek out, as it helps them write better papers. When a paper is due, this will clearly be a priority choice in their spending.

Which company has the better approach for acquiring customers? Both sides have their advantages. Questia has an upfront fee, but at $109.95 per year, it's not too high for college students who have disposable incomes of about $200 per month. The one-time sale justifies the sales cost. The drawback is that people may just wait until they need the service before spending the money and then may balk at the cost. The question for Questia is how many students will buy the service off the Internet.

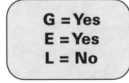

G = Yes
E = No
L = Yes

At 15 to 25 cents a page, Ebrary has an easier entry point than Questia. But the possibility exists that students may only make 15 to 20 copies, which is not much of a sale for the work Ebrary has to do to get the customer, and the one-time sale is no guarantee the students will be back to buy. The question is, will enough students use the service often enough on a pay-as-you-go basis to justify Ebrary's sales expense?

G = Yes
E = Yes
L = No

Both Questia and Ebrary have question mark pricing schemes. They could have also tried other concepts, such as a monthly fee with a 12-month commitment that automatically renews or a lower annual fee with a small per-copy fee. Ultimately, the market will decide which approach works best. Business owners need to be aware of the risks in their concepts and be ready to adjust when necessary.

SIX KEY FACTORS FOR EVALUATING EASY SALES

		Desired	Excellent	Average	Poor
Value to Customer	How Important	Important			
	Competitive Advantage	High			
	Price/Value Relationship	Low			
Customer Acquisition Cost	Entry Points	Many			
	Sales Support Required	Little			
	Promotional Activities	Low			

FIGURE 3-1. GEL factor easy sales checklist

Are You Important to Customers?

Why It's Important

Customers determine value by their standards and not by yours. Those standards have been evolving over the last few years to be more emotional than practical. Think of some of the great sales successes over the last few years—Starbucks, the Palm Pilot, and SUVs. None of these were truly important for customers. But customers wanted them, because those items made them feel better. Partly it was a reward for themselves, partly it said to others that they were important, and partly it was to reinforce their own image of success.

Companies operate in the same way. They want to project a variety of images that could include "breakthrough company," "marketing-driven company," "quality-conscious company," and even "cost-conscious company." Businesses need to project an image to their employees, vendors, customers, and competitors and the image they desire is important.

The marketing reality is that buying is dominated by what buyers feel are their top priorities. People may have only two or three priorities that they can worry about and those are the only ones that drive their buying decisions.

When It's a Key Concern

1. *When the product is sold through a distribution network.* If the product is important to customers and brand loyalty exists, distributors will buy the products customers want.

2. *Practicality is more influential on the customer's buying decision than fun or emotion.* Customers with money in their pocket are willing to buy from anyone products that add fun, but they stick with the tried and true when it is a practical purchase.

3. *Customers aren't confident of the purchasing process.* Confused buyers rarely buy. And confused buyers take the trouble to learn about a product or service only if the benefit is important to them.

4. *Purchases can easily be delayed or postponed.* For example, most of the time a new stereo isn't a necessary purchase; people can take a long time before deciding to buy. You'll waste time chasing customers who keep delaying their purchase decision because the purchase isn't important to them.

5. *You have a limited number of contacts with any one customer.* You may get only one or two times to truly talk to a customer and you need to be to selling something important to the customer if you want the customer to buy quickly.

*M*ost buyers, whether it's business customers or consumers, are worried about only their top two or three priorities. Many entrepreneurs make the mistake of not asking customers if buying their product or one like it is a priority decision. Because they fail to ask, they may mistakenly believe that they have a winner, when it fact what they're offering doesn't meet a desire that's high on the customers' list of priorities.

How to Compensate

1. *Add an emotional context to the purchase decision.* Purchasing a new set of car tires is a practical decision. But Michelin added an emotional context to that decision when it showed a baby in its ads and promotions with the tag line "there's a lot riding on your tires."

2. *Create strong promotional programs to encourage immediate buying.* When your product or service isn't important by itself, you can often create a buying decision by making buyers feel they will miss out if they don't buy right away.

3. *Use testimonials from industry experts or affiliations with other people trusted by customers.* Customers, both consumer and industrial, like to buy winning products, so testimonials can be a big asset.

4. *Target a segment of your customer group where your product or service is most important rather than trying to sell the broad market.*

How Do They Act?

How can you really be sure that your product or service is important? One good barometer is the effort customers are already taking to try and solve the problem. There are many ways you can tell if customers have a strong desire for a certain product or service.

1. Great success for companies currently meeting that desire.

2. High customer attendance at shows or seminars on the topic.

3. High use of consultants and other services to deal with the issue (the Y2K panic).

4. Heavy news coverage and stories.

5. Buyers buying. People started buying bigger homes and SUVs and the market responded.

6. Success in other markets. A retail concept might take off in one area and then spread, such as Staples, starting on the East Coast and then moving into the Midwest.

Your Competitive Advantage

Why It's Important

Customers have options—they can almost always find another product to meet the same need as your product. If you're going to succeed, you must have a strong reason for people to buy your product or service over competing products or services. Here are some of the areas where you can get a competitive advantage:

1. Better support of customers' self-image
2. Best performance
3. More complete solution
4. Top perceived value
5. First with the newest technology
6. Most visual appeal
7. Highest-quality product
8. Best-known product brand
9. Lowest pricing

When It's a Key Concern

1. *A distribution channel is involved in the product.* Distribution channels are more knowledgeable about the differences among products and they evaluate all of the product choices.
2. *Competitors are established in the market.* Buyers feel more comfortable buying from companies they know. With established competitors, a strong advantage is the only way to get noticed.
3. *You have fewer resources than competitors.* Com-panies that can't compete with a marketing budget must rely on their product differentiation to sell products.
4. *Customers can quickly tell which product or service is best.* For example, you can try out two scanners and see that one has better resolution than another.

SUCCESSFUL BUSINESS MODELS

5. Buyers are willing to shop for the best product. Some people visit 10 to 15 furniture stores before buying a sofa. They check out all the product features before buying.

How to Compensate

1. *Add features and/or form partnerships.* A competitive advantage is one tactic for getting buyers to notice you. Another option is to join forces with a partner to either sell a package of products or services or to offer a more complete solution to the customers.

2. *Focus more clearly on a smaller target customer group.* Try to look for customers where your product has distinct advantages and then focus on that group.

3. *Offer convincing proof.* You might do this with test results, testimonials, documented cost savings from customers, or customer evaluations of competing products.

4. *Increase your use of visual images.* People are heavily influenced by first impressions and the visual is a key to that first impression. Having the best-looking package or the best-looking product is a big advantage.

5. *Become a market focal point.* You can sponsor events, conduct classes, be a leader of association committees, or sponsor a trade show or special speaker.

One sure way to guarantee problems in selling your product is to offer the same benefits as everyone else. How many companies targeting businesses have as their primary benefit that they help customers save money? Thousands. Customers quickly learn to avoid messages when they've heard them before.

Perceived Price/Value
Why It's Important

People have a strong sense of what something is worth to them, a value that is determined by their own criteria. If a family takes a vacation to Disney World and the total bill comes to $2,500, will they consider that a great value?

MAKING THE EASY SALE / 33

Some people will consider it a bargain because of Disney World's atmosphere and excitement, while others will resent the high prices and think that they would have been better off taking a camping trip to the mountains for $500. When you consider the perceived value of your product or service, it doesn't matter what the product or service costs to provide or what value you feel it has. It only matters what the target customer perceives the value of your product or service to be.

> *Value-added* is a phrase you'll hear both from bankers and venture capitalists. It refers to services or add-ons that make a product or a service more valuable to customers. Putting a spring on the bows of kids' glasses is a value-added feature, because it makes it more difficult for kids to break their glasses.

When It's a Key Concern

1. *Customers consider the product or service a discretionary purchase.* I see flowers all the time on downtown outdoor malls. I buy some for my wife when I think the price/value is right.
2. *There are many other options for purchasing.* You won't buy a CD if you think the price is too high, because you have both many other places to buy a CD and many other CDs you could buy instead.
3. *Your product isn't well known or is unproven.* People will take a chance on buying a new product if they feel it's a better value than current products, but they won't try a new product if they feel it's overpriced.
4. *Your customers are cost-conscious or value-oriented.* Engineers, accountants, and thrifty people all evaluate their product choices closely.

How to Compensate

1. *Add high-value elements or services.* Better-quality components, stainless steel versus plastic, or an enhanced atmosphere for a store will raise perceived value.
2. *Drop features or benefits for which the perceived value is low.*

3. *Find a cheaper way to produce your product or service.* If you can't add enough value, you may be able to cut your costs so that your perceived value is acceptable to customers.

4. *Totally overhaul your business approach.* You may not be providing enough value to your customers. Successful businesses frequently change their business concept three to four times before finding something that works.

Entry Points Available
Why It's Important

How many ways can people start to buy from you? Those are your entry points. The more entry points you have, the easier it will be for you to find and sell customers.

Here's an example. A copier supplier could just sell or lease a product. That's two entry points. The supplier could also offer a 60-day trial or offer to rent the product. That's two more entry points. The company could also have a Web site and offer its product through an office supply store as an incentive for buying a year-long office supplies contract.

Entry points apply to all businesses. For a manufacturer of consumer products, entry points include anywhere a person can buy the product from stores, catalogs, and Internet sites. For a retailer, the entry points include how people can access the stores: the number of doors, the foot traffic by the store caused by nearby retailers, and the number of people who drive by.

When It's a Key Concern

1. *Your market is highly competitive.* Often the company that gets the sale is just the one with the most or easiest entry points.

When establishing the perceived value for your product, don't ask people what they feel it is worth or what they would pay. Customers almost always state an amount that's much lower than they will pay. Instead, have your customers rank your product or service along with five or six other similar products or services by value. Your perceived value will be close to the products ranked just above and just below your product.

> *O*pportunism works. Many sales people get the order by just calling on the customer on the right day or because they're at a trade show right when the customer is ready to order. Opportunism is simply having a door open when the customer is ready to buy. Having lots of entry points for customers is just another way of being opportunistic.

2. *Customers may elect not to buy your product or service.* Life insurance, water filtration systems, or special phone headsets are all products people can elect not to buy. You have the best chance of encouraging a buying decision by having the product available in many locations and in many different ways.

3. *The sale is to a customer that provides limited revenue opportunities.* These customers don't justify sales and marketing expenses and your best chance of success of a sale is having your product available in many locations.

4. *People have a short buying process.* For example, if I'm going to buy a fishing rod, I wait until I'm getting ready to go fishing and then I buy one at the closest or first store I come to.

How to Compensate

1. *Go into the customer's world.* You need to hold contests, host seminars, be active in associations, and in effect go where customers go.

2. *Form partnerships and alliances to expand your market presence.*

3. *Create a strong prospect follow-up program.* If your customers can't easily run across your products, you can stay after them. Contact management programs like Act or Goldmine help companies set up programs for periodic mailings and follow-up phone calls.

4. *Create an easy-to-sell entry point.* CD- and movie-buying clubs have just two entry points: customers can respond to a direct mail piece and join through the Internet. Those entry points are easy for the customer to use.

Sales Support Required

Why It's Important

A new home, a piece of production equipment, an annuity, and a new, enterprise-wide software package are the type of decision that people make only after extensive sales support, which includes presentations, demonstrations, training, help with installation, and answering repeated calls.

Sales support presents two problems for companies. The first is that it requires a big and expensive sales organization. This cost is overhead and, especially for startups, it can represent an expense that can produce substantial deficits for the first year or two. The second reason is that sales support costs can end up being 25% to 40% of revenue: that expense can take a heavy toll on the bottom line.

When It's a Key Concern

1. *When you have a complex or unknown product.* You need to worry about support anytime the customer needs help making a buying decision.
2. *The sales dollars you can generate from each customer are low.* To succeed, the sales support you can offer based on your profit per sale must be limited.
3. *Your resources are limited.* Sales support costs money, sometimes lots of money, in terms of sales staff, demo products, sales materials, and training.
4. *Your customers are widely scattered.* Complex sales requiring lots of sales support sometimes also typically require multiple sales calls, which are especially costly when customers are scattered.
5. *The purchase is not a high priority for the customer.* Customers tend to put off complex sales; this tendency is even stronger when the purchase is not one of the top two or three priorities for the customers.

*A **cross promotion** describes a joint venture or partnership agreement in which one company promotes another company's service. A car wash that offers a coupon for $5.00 off at a nearby oil change dealership is doing a cross promotion. In return, the oil change dealership might offer a coupon for $3.00 off at the car wash. Other cross promotions include joint newsletters, sharing space at trade shows, or offering package specials.*

How to Compensate

1. *Take responsibility for the complete solution.* Guaranteeing a result that meets the customer's expectations minimizes the need for sales support.

2. *Offer a service rather than a purchase plan.* No worries— that's what the customer wants when a purchase is complex or confusing or difficult. Instead of just selling a product that the customer needs to figure out how to use, you can also provide a service that does the job for the customer.

3. *Set up or use a distribution network.* One of the advantages of distribution networks is that they have more frequent contact with your customer than you do and they can offer sales support at a lower cost.

4. *Offer high sales compensation.* If you have a tough sale, you need the best sales people and you can get them only with generous compensation. Look for experienced salespeople with a history of high earnings.

5. *Enlist the aid of industry experts as part of your marketing team.* They can overcome customer confusion, skepticism, and worry—the big three reasons that a sale becomes difficult.

Promotional Activities Required

Why It's Important

Promotional activities are another item that can be a prohibitive expense. Retail stores in offbeat locations can spend money on big events, advertising, attendance at trade shows, or direct mail campaigns. Other stores will pay the expensive rent of a mall to bring in customers. On the other hand, some businesses have low promotional expenses; some can operate out of homes and simply call on the four big customers in their area. A group of ex-

*M*any companies take it for granted that distributors will push your product once they decide to sell it. That's simply not true. One of the reasons that distributors can build customer loyalty is that they are careful to present customers only products or services in which they have confidence. When using distributors, be sure you take the time to train them so they will push your product aggressively.

Lockheed engineers, for example, started a product design business with just one customer, Lockheed. They had no promotional budget. High promotion costs result in more overhead, higher prices, and generally a riskier business concept.

When It's a Key Concern

1. *Customers are difficult to locate.* You need to promote aggressively when you can't buy a list of customers, don't have events where customers gather, or can't team up with other suppliers serving the same market.

2. *You can't be sure when a customer is going to buy.* Which business this year will be buying new office partitions for an employee expansion? You can spend lots of money when you don't know which customers to concentrate on.

3. *Low to moderate pricing and average sale value.* The more customers to whom you need to promote your product or service in order to generate a profitable sales level, the more you need to be concerned about promotion expense.

4. *You need to establish a new brand or product against established competition.* Getting brand recognition takes a long time, especially if competitors have an entrenched customer base.

5. *You have a new category of product or service.* The toughest job of promotion is when people aren't even aware that your brand or service is available.

How to Compensate

1. *Establish a recurring revenue stream from each customer.* A monthly service produces more sales than a one-time product sale.

2. *Add new products or services that customers need.* Many companies have their own product line but are also distributors for other manufacturers. Companies will also be sales agents for other companies.

3. *Develop tools to attract customer interest early in their buying process.* Classes, seminars, and information Web sites are all ways to find customers well before they're ready to buy.

4. *Create extremely effective promotional materials or visual images.* We live in a visual age and I've found that people are four to five times more likely to remember your product or service if you associate a powerful visual image with it.

5. *Have a distinctive product or service feature that makes your company memorable.* You can cut significantly the number of exposures customers need before buying if you have one unique, dramatic feature or benefit.

Easy Sales Are Hard to Come By

More on Dr. Spock Co., O'Naturals, and Jawroski's Towing and Service. The one point to notice is that a business needs all of the GEL factors for success.

There are six comparison factors:
1. How important the purchase is to customers
2. Your competitive advantage
3. How customers perceive your price/value relationship
4. How many sales entry points you have
5. Sales support required
6. How many promotional activities you'll need

Dr. Spock Co.

The entire premise behind Dr. Spock Co. is that raising children is extremely important to a certain segment of professional parents. That importance is the motivator that drives the business.

Evaluation on the basis of easy sales:

1. Children are important to all parents and bringing children up well is important to a large segment of professional parents of infants. Score: +.

2. Customers' perception of Dr. Spock's competitive advantage over newer authority sources is unclear. Score: -.

3. Customers may not see Dr. Spock as having a strong price/value relationship unless they first value Dr. Spock's advice. Score: -.

4. The company should be able to have a large number of entry points, especially if they should get support from their pamphlets distributed by doctors. Score: +.

5. Sales support of users will be low because of Dr. Spock's name recognition and because the purchase price is relatively low. Score: +.

6. Promotional activities will be needed, especially as the customer base will change each year, but the promotional activities will still be low due to the brand name. Score +.

O'Naturals

O'Naturals founders developed a stronger position for customer value because they started with what they felt was an unmet customer need, healthy fast food. O'Naturals has to deal with two aspects regarding

The best visual images don't focus on your product, but instead on the solution or result for the customer. This helps customers relate the product to their situations. A picture of a kitchen cabinet doesn't connect with a customer, but a glistening remodeled kitchen does. Your visuals should reflect the result customers want when they buy your product.

customer value. The first is whether healthy food is important to O'Naturals customers. The answer is clearly yes. The second is whether or not fast food is important to people that want healthy meals. The jury is certainly out on the second point.

Evaluation on the basis of easy sales:

1. In terms of importance to the customers, healthy food alone rates a +, but healthy fast food is at best an even choice. Score: Even.

2. O'Naturals clearly has a competitive advantage over other fast-food restaurants and an advantage in terms of speed over other healthy-food restaurants or eating at home. Score: +.

3. The customers' view of the O'Naturals price/value relationship depends on how much they value service speed. People willing to take the time to eat healthy food may not place a premium on saving 15 minutes a day at a fast-food restaurant. Score: Even.

4. O'Naturals has only a few restaurants and the number of entrees they can offer will be limited because they're fast-food restaurants. Score: -.

5. Sales support will be important for O'Naturals as it will need to reinforce on each customer visit that it's serving healthy food. The positive point for O'Naturals is that it should be inexpensive to offer that support, with placards on the table and information in the restaurant. Score: +.

6. Promotional activities will be expensive for O'Naturals. While word-of-mouth advertising might work for dedicated healthy eaters, promotion will probably be needed for people with only a mild interest in healthy foods. Score: -.

Jawroski's Towing and Service

Jawroski's will be judged by how effectively the employees solve the customers' problem, the quality of their service, and how their price compares with the competitors. If they do well by those three criteria, customers will keep coming back and word-of-mouth advertising will carry the business.

Evaluation on the basis of easy sales:

1. Car repair is obviously important: if your car is not working, you need it fixed. Score: +.

2. Jawroski's has built its competitive advantage around its high-test equipment and its ability to repairs cars right the first time. This is important to its fleet customers and people in its nearby upscale neighborhoods. All of Jawroski's competitors are smaller shops with less technology. Score: +.

3. Jawroski's customers value getting results above all else, so they perceive that Jawroski's has a strong price/value relationship. Score: +.

4 Jawroski's number of entry points is limited, but the company's ideal location on a busy street compensates. Score: +.

5. Jawroski's sales support is simply giving good service so that cars work. Jawroski's high-technology garage and the owner's commitment to keeping his employees well trained give Jawroski's all the sales support it needs. Score: +.

6. Jawroski's depends on its location for promotion. But it can also generate low-cost promotions in the neighborhood by sponsoring sports teams, allowing high school organizations to hold car washes on its site, and doing inexpensive neighborhood mailings. Score: +.

The Buying Binge

ADC Telecommunications is one of the market leaders in fiber optic technologies for the telecommunications and computer industries. In the late 1990s and early 2000s, ADC purchased several companies that provided products that were complementary to its own. ADC was able to cut its cost of acquiring customers dramatically in several ways because of a bigger product line:

1. *Adds entry points, especially in equipment markets.* ADC's customers need many products to achieve a solution to their needs. By expanding its product line, ADC improved the chances that a customer would call for at least one product.

2. *Cuts sales support costs for each product line.* Customers are looking for a complete integration solution. A broader product line allows ADC to consolidate its whole product line into its training and demonstration programs.

3. *Makes promotional programs more effective.* The more complete your solution, the more your messages and promotional programs will interest potential customers.

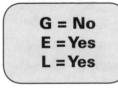

G = No
E = Yes
L = Yes

ADC unfortunately fell on hard times in 2001 and 2002, when its customers' market dried up. But the company is poised for a strong comeback once the market recovers.

BUILDING A LONG FUTURE

DOING WHAT'S NECCESSARY TO ENSURE LONG LIFE ◀

A long future depends on money, how much you need to invest, how much you make from every sale, and how much you need to stay in business. The most important factor is probably profits from every sale, but even profitable companies can be waylaid if they need too much investment. Even a business with a great concept can have unpredictable costs such as an unexpected lawsuit, a sudden price increase from a key vendor; or high promotional expenses in response to an aggressive competitor. A business can also find itself faced with unexpected investments required to meet a competitive market. A business ideally set up for long life has margins high enough to absorb unexpected costs and requires just modest investments to adjust to market and competitive changes.

Nothing Comes Easy

GiftCertificates.com had a simple business concept. It would be a Web site where people could easily buy gift cer-

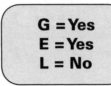

G = Yes
E = Yes
L = No

tificates from a wide variety of retailers. The company set up 4,000 corporate clients and partnerships with 700 merchants, including major retailers like Bloomingdale's. The company had high upfront costs setting up, but that was to be expected. The problem is having high margins in the face of competitive pressures and high ongoing investment to hold onto the business.

The first problem was smaller competitors offering the same package of services for lower prices. GiftCertificates.com responded by buying out two of the bigger competitors, GiftSpot.com and GiftPoint.com, acquisitions that brought the company's debt load up to $90 million. Next the company had to worry about big portal sites like AOL and Yahoo. Locking the big sites into GiftCertificates.com is difficult when AOL and Yahoo can offer the same service if GiftCertificates.com is successful. The company has responded by repeatedly going back to the market for additional capital to promote themselves. But can GiftCertificate.com survive? Their only chance is to hold onto market share by heavy and repeated expenditures to buy off competitors, promote the site to potential customers and keep a presence on the major portals.

SIX KEY FACTORS FOR EVALUATING LONG LIFE

		Desired	Excellent	Average	Poor
Profit per Sale	Margins	High			
	Up-Selling and Cross-Selling	Much			
	Ongoing Product Costs	Low			
Investment Required	To Enter Business	Low			
	To Keep Market Share	Low			
	To Stay on the Cutting Low Edge	Low			

FIGURE 4-1. GEL factor long life checklist

Healthy Margins

Why It's Important

Healthy margins with adequate sales are by far the number one indicator of a healthy company. When I started in business I could never understand why finance people had so much power in a company. After all, I thought, they don't do anything constructive. But I've since learned that I was wrong. Since companies often survive on a profit of 2 to 5% on sales, a few percentage points difference in margin can make all the difference in the world between making and losing money. Controlling margins is one of the most effective ways to determine just how successful a company will be.

When It's a Key Concern

1. *Always.* What about the old adage we'll make up a low margin with high volume? Baloney. Wal-Mart doesn't have low margins. They have low prices

because they have the buying volume to drive down the prices they pay. The fact is that the strategy of low margins and high volume is a risky strategy. You incur large upfront costs to generate high volume, and if the demand shifts even slightly those high costs will be a huge anchor on your profitability.

How to Compensate

1. *Add more value.* Companies that match each other's pricing typically end up losing money. The better approach is to find out what customers really want and than provide that.

2. *Cut manufacturing costs.* A company with a sustainable advantage in product costing is almost impossible to defeat.

3. *Find another method of distribution.* Sometimes low margins are caused by distribution costs. For example if you sell to a wholesaler that sells to a distributor that sells to a retailer you'll only be receiving a fraction of the final retail price. It's not always clear that one or more of these steps in the chain is adding that much value in getting the products to customers. Be aware of that.

4. *Choose another customer group.* You need to find someone who finds more value in your products or service than your current customer group.

5. *Lower your overhead structure.* Overhead is a heavy burden for every company, and you need to check it periodically, whether its rent, phone bills, or computer reports to keep costs in line.

Service companies and retail stores also have costs that they should evaluate constantly. A maternity shop may decide to only keep one size of each garment on the floor with off-site warehousing to keep down inventory costs. Service companies may have high rent, or they may have too many of their employees in non-sales positions.

Up-Selling and Cross-Selling

Why It's Important

Building customer trust is time consuming and expensive. Once you have it, each subsequent sale is easier to make than the last. This is one of the main reasons that people use manufacturers' representatives and distributors. They have already built a bond with customers. Additional sales to an existing customer base are much easier to make than sales to new customers. Businesses that can cross-sell or up-sell have a much better chance of improving their profits per customer.

When It's a Key Concern

1. *A purchase is rarely made.* People buy a refrigerator once every ten years. An appliance store can make much more money if they can add significantly to the customer's purchase with an up-sell or cross-sell. The extra sale has to be made on the spot since the customer might not come back for another 10 years.

2. *The sales costs are high relative to the purchase price.* All products or services have a certain value to the customer that limit what you can charge. The amount might not cover your sales cost unless you can increase your profit with additional sales.

3. *Future customer contact is unlikely.* When you call up to order a product from a TV commercial you are unlikely to call that company again.

4. *The customer makes a high priority purchase.* Customers are often responsive to an up-sell or cross-sell when they are making what is for them a high priority purchase.

Cross-sell refers to selling another type product to the same customer. For example, a cross-sell for a retailer of upscale audio equipment might be big screen TVs or a car audio system. An **up-sale** is adding features to an already existing purchase. A TV retailer for example, would consider a "sound around" stereo system to be an up-sell because it is an upgrade of a TV purchase.

How to Compensate

1. *Add a consumable component to your sales mix.* Water softeners manufacturers deliver salt and put it into water softeners. Software companies charge a monthly lease fee for software and others have a monthly maintenance fee.

2. *Sell private label products.* Find products that complement yours or are a natural up-sell or cross-sell and then arrange to sell it under your name. This is especially effective if the private label product is a consumable product.

3. *Combine ongoing with one-time services.* An air conditioning service company for industrial buildings might include yearly cleaning of the vents, shut-down and start-up services, and even air quality monitoring services.

4. *Restrict your sales to high yield customers.* You can't afford to try and sell to every potential customer. Find the customers that you can sell to profitably and then just forget about the others.

Ongoing Product Costs

Why It's Important

A supplier of playground equipment to children's day care centers knows that his customers have steady turnover, and the supplier needs to expect numerous follow up calls and inquiries over the life of the equipment. Garden shops know that trees they sell will die quickly and that they will have to be replaced. Computer equipment manufacturers know that changes in computer hardware and software will necessitate follow-up support for their equipment. In every case, the supplier may need to provide services at no charge to the customer, but the service is certainly not free to the supplier. Too many ongoing costs of a sale will certainly kill a company's products and make a sale that is at first glance profitable, unprofitable.

When It's a Key Concern

1. *There is turnover among people using your product.* An advertising agency will have high costs if the main contact for its customers keeps changing. The agency will need to offer more personal contact and more explanations to ensure they don't lose the account.

2. *Your product or service interfaces with many other products or services.* You may need to offer new connections, or you might need to integrate your equipment with other new products offered after the introduction of your product.

3. *The market you compete in has rapid changes.* Changes in the market typically mean your customers may be using your product in different ways. They'll be contacting you for updates on how to use your products, and you may need to provide adjustments to the products or services you've provided.

4. *Customers don't have the knowledge to adjust for or correct small problems.* When something small goes wrong with a lawnmower most homeowners know how to fix it. Customers don't do that when they are unfamiliar with a product.

5. *Your product or service replaces a well-know product.* Established products typically have all of their kinks worked out and run smoothly for customers. Customers expect a new product to work just as smoothly, which rarely happens with a new product.

*E*ntrepreneurs tend to be optimists and they frequently wear rose-colored glasses when someone brings up a potential negative for their business. Don't ignore problems. Instead try and talk to other people in your business at trade shows or association meetings and see what type of costs they are incurring. It's likely your costs will be similar. You might not like the answer, but at least you'll be prepared.

How to Compensate

1. *Set your customer's expectations.* Don't act as if your product or service is "drop and run" (you sell it and never come back) if in fact you know the customer will need a fairly large amount of ongoing product support.
2. *Create online or ongoing training and service.* Let the customer know up front that you have ongoing training and service programs. Have the staff in place to execute those programs, and plan these expenses in your budget and the price of your offering.
3. *Plan product upgrades that track industry changes.* Hewlett Packard is a good example of a company that anticipates industry changes and has the product upgrades available right when their customers need them.
4. *Make accessibility to solutions easy for customers with problems.* Have solutions to problems prepared in

> *Ongoing product support doesn't have to be free. You can charge for it and make a profit. I feel one of the biggest mistakes companies make is to try to provide a minimal level of support that only irritates the customer. Those companies would be much better off giving customers exactly what they want and charging for it.*

Big Steps Often Work

One of the big problems many companies have when dealing with cost issues and particularly margin issues is that they think incrementally. That may work to tweak a business just a few margin points, but you should also consider big radical moves. I worked with a $30-million company that sold products to the dental industry. The company made money most years, but the profits were always modest. The company had a large administrative staff, big marketing and R&D departments, and three manufacturing plants.

Looking at the customer base the company found that about 40% of its customers were very loyal. The rest of the customer base had varying degrees of loyalty, but the last 20%, were not only not loyal, they were expensive to sell to as they required lots of product support. The company's strategy was to cut non-manufacturing office personnel by 80% and just sell to its loyal and semi-loyal base. Sales dropped about 25%, but profits went up over 800%. Incremental thinking would never have come to this conclusion. Consider your business from all angles to find solutions to profitability problems.

advance that you can send to customers with problems. Many people will fix a problem themselves if you tell them how to do it.

Costs of Entering the Market

Why It's Important

Start-up costs include manufacturing costs, setting up the company, and launching a marketing and sales campaign. The main concern for most people is just having enough money to launch the business. But from a GEL factor perspective its not just how much money, after all, companies raise hundreds of millions of dollars in initial investments, its how much money will the investment make. Ideally you want the annual market sales potential to be at least 10 times the amount of the investment required. Otherwise you have to question whether or not the investment is worth the risk of the business failing.

When It's a Key Concern

The amount of investment versus the market potential is always key, but in some cases it is of critical importance.

1. *You have an untested business concept.* New business concepts have plenty of kinks and a business's chance of success is in doubt if the up-front investment is high and you can't be sure when the business will turn a profit.

2. *The product life cycle is short.* A short product life cycle means that a company has to get its investment back in a big hurry, which can be hard to do with a big initial investment.

3. *You don't have access to significant resources.* You and your inner circle of initial investors have to provide a significant share of the start-up capital. If you are low

*T*oo often new entrepreneurs assume that competitors will just keep on operating the way they always have even if they lose market share. Competitors do respond, sometimes decisively, when a competitor gains an advantage. Businesses need a feature that gives it a sustainable advantage, one competitors can't easily duplicate, to succeed. For example, start-up budget airlines quickly attract price competition from large airlines that have led to the demise of these start-ups.

on funds, pick a project that only requires a modest up-front investment.

4. *You have a major competitor.* You'll need to provide twice as muchf service for the same price as the big competitor because customers are just as skeptical of newcomers as they are comfortable with a major supplier.

How to Compensate

1. *Partner up with major players.* Cut your investment by partnering with another company and using its resources. You might have a partner handle all of your administrative functions, use their salesforce, or simply use the partner's name for credibility.

2. *Pre-sell contracts to major prospects.* You will reduce your risk if you convince three or four customers to sign a contract before you make the initial investment. Distributors, retailers, and buyers will often place an order if you offer the right incentives and have an innovative product or service.

3. *Quickly corner a segment of the market.* With a big up-front investment you want to avoid a lengthy period waiting for sales. One tactic is to focus on a small part of the market to generate a solid, though small sales base.

4. *Have an innovative promotional or sales strategy.* You can set up a sales, distribution, or promotional program to lock up customers such as selling a product based on a monthly service charge rather than a standard sales price.

5. *Outsource high cost operations.* Manufacturing, promotion, and staffing require the biggest up-front costs and these functions can be outsourced to other com-

panies. You can also share administrative costs and overhead expenses by sharing office space.

Costs to Hold onto Market Share

Why It's Important

The company story box at the beginning of this chapter talked about GiftCertificates.com. Buying market share for six months is great if the edge you generate will sustain itself afterwards with a much lower promotional level. If it won't, the company will have trouble surviving. Buying market share with lower prices is typically a short-lived strategy because competitors will respond with their own low prices. The same is true with promotions and sales efforts. The competitors can match you and then your only recourse is to try and outspend your rivals.

When It's a Key Concern

1. *Customers don't perceive differences between products.* Levi's held major market share in the jeans market for years with heavy promotion. Then their promotional efforts slowed down, and they immediately lost market share.
2. *Large, established competitors are already in the market.* Big companies have their own promotional war chest that you have to compete against to get noticed.
3. *Alternative low cost marketing methods (events, shows, association and user groups) are not viable.* Customers have a keen interest in some product categories, such as wedding dresses, or Internet marketing, and they will come to events and notice new market entrees.
4. *You can't gain an advantage with sales and/or distribution tactics.* Offering the highest commissions, setting up franchises or distributorships, signing exclusive

Alternative marketing tactics work best when a product or service is new and unusual. You don't, however, have to have a radically new segment to use this tactic. Garden stores that offer classes in English rock gardens are offering a slight twist that will generate customer interest. Paint and home improvement stores are taking the same tact with faux finishing classes, merchandise, and displays.

agreements with key distribution outlets, and signing customers up to long-term contracts are all ways to minimize promotional expenses.

5   *Marketing and promotion costs are high.* Marketing to teenagers is expensive. Advertising on TV or in teen-oriented magazines costs lots of money as does sponsoring rock shows or other events.

How to Compensate

1. *Find more effective ways to differentiate your product.* Find one important desire of your customers and then create a feature or benefit that customers can easily notice.

2. *Compete only in segments where your product is differentiated.* Stop trying to sell to markets where your costs are high and competition stiff because prospects can't see your advantage.

3. *Form partnerships to offer a better customer solution.* Customers love to buy a "plug and play" solution—something that works immediately. Once you understand the solution the customer wants, you'll find that there are plenty of potential partners available.

4. *Go out of the box with your name and promotion strategy.* Kinetix was a small computer animation company that put the Dancing Baby out for free on the Web. The concept was a huge hit and the company had a million dollar promotional campaign that was virtually free.

5. *Refocus on a smaller market segment that you can afford.* Companies have to be sure they get a return on the money they spend, and sometimes that means they have to go after a small market where their promotional efforts will have an impact.

Features are the specific tasks or image your product or service offers. **Benefits** are why those features are important to the customer. An automatic transmission on a car is a feature. The benefit is that people don't have to shift gears manually. Benefits are more important than features, but what customers actually buy is a solution, which in this case is an easy-to-drive car. So think in terms of solutions rather than benefits or even features.

Costs to Stay on the Cutting Edge

Why It's Important

Nothing succeeds like having the newest, best products and services that everyone wants. The demand for the product brings you the promotional recognition you need without having to pay for it. If you are not on the cutting edge, not only are you at a distinct disadvantage when selling every customer, but you also are faced with the need for a much higher promotional budget. Cell phones are a good example. When they first came out there were just a few competitors with state of the art products, and those companies had very small promotional and advertising budgets. They didn't need to advertise because people knew about the products from magazines and newspaper stories. Today consumers don't differentiate cellular phones that well, and companies have to advertise heavily.

When It's a Key Concern

1. *Customers are gadget or new technology lovers.* These customers know what's happening in the market, and they won't stay with you even one week if someone else introduces the latest gadget.

2. *Customers rely on cutting edge products for status.* Salespeople, business executives, and others always want the latest electronic gadget so they look like they are on the cutting edge.

3. *New technology significantly reduces costs or raises productivity.* Siebel Systems made its mark with customer relationship management software. That product increased the effectiveness of the salesforce and made the company more money. State of the art meant more productivity and more profits for the users.

4. *Current technology has well-known deficiencies.* Diesel truck technology has two big deficiencies: they are big-time polluters, and they have low gas mileage. Truck owners immediately look at new products that can minimize those problems, providing they have a minimal cost.

5. *Rapid product or service changes occur in the industry.* This applies to most markets today. The pace of product change and improvement has never been higher.

How to Compensate

1. *Become tightly affiliated with a segment of the target market.* You can't stay on the cutting edge of development if you don't have a great understanding of your customers' current and upcoming needs.

2. *Use a customer advisor group to keep ahead of the market trends.* Meeting with key customers or prospects three to four times a year will help you keep a firm grasp of what customers want.

3. *Utilize outside product design sources.* Some companies have a relationship with outside inventors. Explain to the outside sources, inventors or product designers about your upcoming needs and offer to pay a royalty on any products they develop that are introduced.

When You Don't Need Customer Input

Many executives feel they don't need customer input. That's true when a company knows:

1. What solution every customer wants.
2. The customer's priorities for each aspect of the solution.
3. All the upcoming changes from products or services the solution interacts with.
4. New and emerging trends in the customer's world that will impact their solution.
5. Nobody can know all this all the time. You need customer input.

4. *Focus spending on product development.* If the cutting edge is where your company belongs, you are often far better off spending your efforts developing new products or services than you are spending money setting up a well-oiled administrative staff.

Living Long

This is our continuing review of three companies: Dr. Spock Co., O'Naturals, and Jawroski's Towing and Service. The one point to notice is that every business needs all of the GEL factors for success.

This time, we'll compare these factors:

1. The health of margins
2. The amount of up-selling and cross-selling available
3. The size of ongoing product support
4. Cost to enter the business
5. Cost to keep market share
6. Cost to stay on the cutting edge.

Dr. Spock Co.

Publishing has large fixed costs in producing the first unit, and then low costs to produce more copies. The situation is much better in e-publishing where there are no up-front print costs. The nice point of Dr. Spock's concept is that while the up-front costs are high, future costs should be modest as the company should generate up-sells and cross-sells.

Evaluation of Dr. Spock's potential for long life:

1. Dr. Spock will have high margins for everything they sell once they overcome their up-front costs. Score: +.

2. People who adopt the Dr. Spock approach are likely to buy many products and services as their children go through their early years. Score: +.

3. One nice aspect of the publishing costs is that there are few ongoing sales costs except returns. Many of Dr. Spock's products and services will be sold over the Internet where return costs will be low. Score: +.

4. The up-front investment is high but certainly justified based on the Dr. Spock brand name and the large potential market. Score: +.

5. Funding to hold market share, based on the company's evaluation of the acceptance of Dr. Spock, should be relatively low. Score: +.

6. Dr. Spock won't need to spend money to stay on the market edge as children and their needs don't change. The company's only significant spending, if they choose to do it, would be research showing Dr. Spock is still relevant. Score: +.

O'Naturals

Many fast food restaurants have struggled over the years because the profit per sale is low. After all one of the dominating benefits of fast food is low prices. Restaurants depend on volume, and volume at every meal. Fast food restaurants try cross-selling and up-selling with upsizing and desserts, but they only add modestly to sales. All three costs are a problem at fast food chains as it is tough to compete with McDonalds.

Evaluation of O'Naturals' potential for long life:

1. Margins at fast food restaurants like O'Naturals are significantly lower than traditional restaurants. Score: -.

2. Cross-selling at a restaurant is usually associated with selling more food, which is not likely with a customer base of people who watch what they eat. One smart option O'Naturals is pursuing is family meals to take home similar to Boston Market. Score: Even.

3. Follow-up costs are extremely low at a restaurant as the people consume the product. Score: +.

4. The initial investment is high, but like Dr. Spock, it is justified by the significant size of the market. Score: +.

5. Funding to hold market share is probably out of reach of most start-up companies if the natural fast food restaurant concept takes off. The company's position can usually be salvaged by selling out to a well-funded company. Score: Even.

6. The investment required for new food entrees or the occasional remodeling is small, but promoting those changes is high. Score: -.

Jawroski's Towing and Service

One thing consumers soon learn is that there is always lots of maintenance that can be done on a car, and customers have to get the repair work done right. That is great for Jawroski's as they have lots of possibilities for selling more services. Jawroski's has a high up-front investment with its high tech diagnostic equipment, but once it's in, ongoing costs are modest.

Evaluation of Jawroski's potential for long life:

1. Auto repair shops typically have strong margins as long as their mechanics can complete work in a timely manner. Score: +.

2. Up-selling and cross-selling are naturals with mechanics who both want to sell more services but also want customers to be aware of other problems in case the car suffers another quick breakdown. Score: +.

3. Jawroski has to be careful to control its service quality and to control customers' expectations of the work performed in order to keep follow up sales costs down. Score: Even.

4. It's not inexpensive to open up a car repair facility, but the cost is justified by the market size and the high profit margins of an auto repair shop. Score: +.

5. Funding to hold market share is usually not a problem for car repairs because consumers like to use a shop either by their home or where they work. There is a danger in losing fleet business, but Jawroski's has a big head start there as it already holds the business and has an excellent reputation. Score: +.

6. Auto repair shops have to invest to stay on the cutting edge, but the expense is usually minimal as all the major companies offer training classes and assist shops in getting the equipment needed for the new cars they introduce. Score: +.

Don't Level the Field

G = Yes
E = Yes
L = Yes

ProSavvy is a dot-com company that started from a $10,000 investment and has grown to serve over 17,000 clients with almost 100 employees. ProSavvy is an Internet matchmaker between consulting firms and end users, which include *Fortune* 500 companies like Texaco and Hasbro. At first glance ProSavvy doesn't seem to be much different than GiftCertificates.com. They have competition from Guru.com and other sites that connect consultants and companies and endless promotion seemed to be in their future.

But ProSavvy realized that they would only succeed by staying on the cutting edge. They realized that firms had hundreds of consultants to choose from, but that they didn't always know the right consultant to choose. ProSavvy stood out from the competition by developing Internet-based tools and standards that helped companies select the right consultant for the right price for their firm. ProSavvy succeeded with one of marketing's basic lessons, customers will locate you when you give them exactly what they want. Follow ProSavvy's approach for success. Don't try to out promote the competition. Instead offer what prospects perceive to be a better package of services.

EVALUATING YOUR CONCEPT

DO CUSTOMERS WANT WHAT YOU HAVE TO SELL? ◀

*T*he reason I've heard most from business owners for not doing a business plan is that things change too fast and a business plan is obsolete after just a few months. The business owners have a point. Plans do constantly change.

But the fact that things change is the very reason business owners need to do GEL factor analysis frequently. Whether they end up writing a plan then is not as important as doing an analysis. I recommend you take a close look at your business concept, see its flaws, and then correct them as your business changes.

The big advantage of this approach is that flaws you find in your business concept can be corrected before they cost you any money. Those entrepreneurs writing a plan before doing a GEL factor analysis will probably eventually make the same changes that an entrepreneur doing a GEL factor analysis will make. But they'll make them only after they've learned by failing—a lesson that can be very expensive.

There are three steps involved in evaluating your concept:

1. Fill in your checklists.
2. Readjust your strategy.
3. Do the final tally.

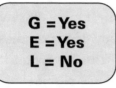

G = Yes
E = Yes
L = No

EC Outlook's experience is typical of new startups: they frequently need to change their business model in order to succeed. The trick is to find the right model without spending a lot of money. Hopefully this chapter will help you make the changes you need without exhausting your resources.

Not Always the First Choice

EC Outlook of Houston, Texas has been chosen as one of *Inbound Logistics Magazine*'s Top 100 Logistics IT Providers, one of *Upside Magazine*'s Hot 100 Companies, and one of *Computerworld*'s top 100 emerging companies to watch. EC Outlook provides e-business connectivity solutions—and it's thriving today in the age of dot-bombs.

EC Outlook is succeeding today, but it's actually on its fourth business model concept. The company demonstrates the wisdom of the old adage, "If at first you don't succeed, try, try again." EC Outlook technology is a solution for the problem of connecting companies, with widely varying internal software, through e-marketplaces and e-transactions. EC Outlook's solution is a translation package that converts files from varying formats into a format a communication partner can read.

EC Outlook's first idea was to sell its products to big companies. But that sale, and subsequent product support, was too complicated and expensive. Plan two was to provide conversion services and software to small companies. In this case, the amount of effort to sell to small customers was too much for the revenue generated by the sales. The third choice was to sell a service to large companies that would convert incoming and outgoing data to and from small and midsize vendors that didn't have conversion capabilities. This was a big sale and relatively easy, as it eliminated a big problem for big companies, how to seamlessly connect to small and midsize vendors that have minimal technology capability.

This model was successful for the company and it allowed it to move to a fourth business model, where it both provides conversion service and sells its conversion products.

Fill in Your Checklists

The first step in evaluating your concept is to fill in the checklists at the end of this chapter. As you're filling in these checklists, don't look at them as a matter of pass or fail. They're a starting point for fine-tuning your business concept, for adjusting the model to make it more effective. The next section of the chapter covers how to make adjustments when necessary. You may need to go through the checklist process several times, so you have permission to copy the checklists for those multiple uses.

Remember: these checklists are used to help you create a winning strategy for your firm. Grading your model too high will only hurt you in the long run.

Figure 5-1, GEL factor checklist, will give you an initial assessment of your concept. Objectively evaluate each point on the chart and check the box. For any of the key determinants in the business model evaluation in which your model rates a grade of "average" or "poor," consider compensating tactics.

Figure 5-2, compensating tactics, is a chart where you can list ways to compensate for the weak points of your business, any key element rated as "average" or "poor." A "poor" element needs one or more highly effective compensating tactics; an "average" element might get by with a mildly effective tactic or even without any compensating tactic.

I recommend that you do a little brainstorming exercise before filling out this chart. List at least four to five possible compensating tactics for each element where you rate your performance "average" or "poor." Next, let those tactics set for two to three days. Then, look at them again and try to list two to three other tactics you could use. Finally, wait another two days and choose the tactics you might consider using.

Figure 5-3, preliminary evaluation form, provides an easy way for you to rate how you stand in regard to each element of the successful business model criteria. The "Concern" column is for weak elements of your business model where you can't implement a compensating tactic or where you can't be sure your compensating tactic will work. Of course you'd like all of your checkmarks to be in the "winner" column, but I've never seen a concept have a winning rating in every category. I've also never seen a business model that didn't have at least one concern. But you definitely want your checkmarks to be clustered down the left side of the columns of this chart.

Figure 5-4 is a final evaluation form. I believe that, in order to succeed, three of the six categories must be winners and three must not be concerns. These are the dominating elements that must come first in your analysis. Once you've met those criteria, you should just list your winners and concerns and be sure that you have at least three or four elements that are winners for every element that is a concern.

Most businesses I've worked with can't effectively implement more than three compensating tactics. You need to choose your tactics carefully, both in terms of what concerns you want to address and in terms of which tactics will have the most impact on your business. Consult with at least three or four customers to help you choose the right tactics. They will know which tactics will best help you overcome weaknesses in your business model.

Readjust Your Strategy

I've found you can correct problems in your business model by evaluating four areas of your business strategy:

1. Change target customers.
2. Change the value/importance to customers.
3. Change the sales/distribution strategy.
4. Change how the product/service is produced.

You may need changes in one area or you may decide to change all four. Try to make as few adjustments as possible, however, since a change in one area could create unanticipated concerns in other categories. For example, a change in your target customer could create a dramatic negative shift in your company's value proposition to customers.

Change Target Customers

You might need to look for new target customers for a wide number of reasons, including the following:

- You can't find enough of them.
- They don't spend freely.
- Your product isn't important enough to them.
- They are hard to acquire.
- They require too much sales support.

You simply cannot change a customer group's behavior, perceptions, or tendencies.

Change the Value/Importance to Customers

If you have the right customer group and the customers just aren't buying, you can do any or all of the following:

- Add features and/or services.
- Become a solution.
- Increase your competitive advantage.

The secret to figuring out how to change value and/or importance to customers is to understand what customers really want, the reasons why they buy. You need firsthand customer input and not just pull together what you feel customers want. This is especially true for establishing a competitive advantage. You have an advantage only if you are offering features or solutions that count with the customers.

A simple way to get this information is to make up six to eight product or service offerings with different features and with varying progress toward a solution. You may need to do brochures for each product or service. Then ask customers these questions:

1. What was your first consideration when you evaluated each product?
2. What product would you rank first? Why?
3. What product would you rank last? Why?
4. What features/services would you like to see added?
5. What features/services would you like to see dropped?

Change the Sales/Distribution Strategy

Sales and distribution strategy is probably the most important characteristic of any marketing program. It's also the category where you have far and away the most options. I've listed next some of the major problems you can correct with sales and distribution and some of the corrective measures you can take. Some of these problems can also be addressed with product feature changes.

1. Customers are hard to locate. Correction—sell through other companies or distributors that have already located these customers.
2. Customers require high sales or ongoing product support. Correction—sell through dealer networks or set up a franchisee network to provide the support required.
3. Customers don't perceive your product or service as being important. Correction—sell through other manufacturers or set up a network where a total solution is provided.
4. Customers make a slow decision. Correction—sell through a network where your product is part of a more important choice.

Change How the Product/Service Is Produced

In some cases, your model might have costs that are too

> *One of the biggest negatives I've ever heard from a venture capitalist about an entrepreneurs is that they are "married to their idea"—which translates into "The entrepreneurs aren't going to listen to advice or make the changes necessary to make their business succeed." The chances of creating the ideal business model right from the start are slim. It's crucial for your success to evaluate and adjust your concept.*

high resulting in margins that are just too low. For example, a software consulting service could have a complete staff, which is a high-cost option, or it might only have a few project managers on staff and then hire the independent contractors it needs for each job, which is a lower-cost option. Manufacturers in the U.S. frequently move production to lower-cost manufacturing outlets, either elsewhere in the country or overseas.

Do the Final Tally

Once you've made the final tally, you simply need to go back to the section, "Fill in Your Checklists." Recheck your score to be sure your score is high enough. Once it is, wait at least one week and go over your business model again. With a fresh look you might be able to get a few more ideas on how your model could be further improved. Check your business model score at least every six months. You'll find out new things from the marketplace that might help you further refine your model.

Spending Rises Exponentially

I've found over the past 30 years that there is one business fact no one likes to discuss. That fact is that as your concept, solution, or tactic moves away from the ideal, your spending to make that tactic effective increases at what appears to exponential rates. That is, if an ideal tactic takes $10 to implement, then even a modestly less ideal tactic takes anywhere from $50 to $100 to implement with equal effectiveness.

The tendency for many people is to gloss over deficiencies in their model and throw in compensating tactics. You should be cautious about compensating tactics, as it's difficult for any company to implement more than two or three of them effectively. A better solution is to keep reworking your business concept until you have one that better meets the successful business model criteria. My experience is that compensating tactics will, at the very best, be only half as effective as changing the model so that it meets the success criteria.

		Desired	Excellent	Average	Poor	Compensating Tactics	
						Yes	No
GREAT CUSTOMERS							
Customer Characteristics	Number	High					
	Ease of Finding	Easy					
	Spending Patterns	Prolific					
Customer Value to Company	$ Value of Sale	High					
	Repeat Sales	Many					
	Ongoing Sales Support	Low					
EASY SALES							
Value to Customer	How Important	Important					
	Competitive Advantage	High					
	Price/Value Relationship	Low					
Customer Acquisition Cost	Entry Points	Many					
	Sales Support Required	Little					
	Promotional Activities	Low					
LONG LIFE							
Profit per Sale	Margins	High					
	Up-Selling and Cross-Selling	Much					
	Ongoing Product Costs	Low					
Investment Required	To Enter Business	Low					
	To Keep Market Share	Low					
	To Stay on the Cutting Edge	Low					

FIGURE 5-1. GEL factor checklist

		List Compensating Tactics	Effectiveness		
			1	2	3
GREAT CUSTOMERS					
Customer Characteristics	Number				
	Ease of Finding				
	Spending Patterns				
Customer Value to Company	$ Value of Sale				
	Repeat Sales				
	Ongoing Sales Support				
EASY SALES					
Value to Customer	How Important				
	Competitive Advantage				
	Price/Value Relationship				
Customer Acquisition Cost	Entry Points				
	Sales Support Required				
	Promotional Activities				
LONG LIFE					
Profit per Sale	Margins				
	Up-Selling and Cross-Selling				
	Ongoing Product Costs				
Investment Required	To Enter Business				
	To Keep Market Share				
	To Stay on the Cutting Edge				

FIGURE 5-2. Compensating tactics

		Winner	Average	Corrected	Concern
GREAT CUSTOMERS					
Customer Characteristics	Number				
	Ease of Finding				
	Spending Patterns				
Customer Value to Company	$ Value of Sale				
	Repeat Sales				
	Ongoing Sales Support				
EASY SALES					
Value to Customer	How Important				
	Competitive Advantage				
	Price/Value Relationship				
Customer Acquisition Cost	Entry Points				
	Sales Support Required				
	Promotional Activities				
LONG LIFE					
Profit per Sale	Margins				
	Up-Selling and Cross-Selling				
	Ongoing Product Costs				
Investment Required	To Enter Business				
	To Keep Market Share				
	To Stay on the Cutting Edge				

FIGURE 5-3. Preliminary evaluation form

Must Have Winners		
Customers—Ease of Finding	_____Yes	All must be checked Yes or the model is flawed.
Value to Customer—Price/Value Relationship	_____Yes	
Profit per Sale—Margins	_____Yes	
Must Not Be a Concern		
Customers—Spending Patterns	_____No	All must be checked No or the model is flawed.
Customer Value to Company—Ongoing Sales Support	_____No	
Investment Required—To Keep Market Share	_____No	

Winners	Concerns
1._____	1._____
2._____	2._____
3._____	3._____
4._____	4._____
5._____	5._____
6._____	6._____
7._____	7._____
8._____	8._____
9._____	9._____

Winners need to outnumber concerns by three to one in order to proceed.

FIGURE 5-4. Final evaluation form

▲ ▲ ▲

THE GEL FACTORS

BUSINESS CONCEPT ANALYSIS: CASE STUDIES

GEL FACTOR ANALYSIS

RETAIL, MANUFACTURING, AND SERVICE

Retail Company: AutoFun—Almost but Not Quite Right

AutoFun was a small chain of auto accessories stores that stayed in business about three years. The company offered fun items for the cars, including neon light license plate holders, car stereos, seat covers, bike racks, funny gizmos for the top of the antennas, and car seat covers.

The company's founders felt that their competitive advantage was that no other store concentrated just on fun auto accessories. There are tons of auto parts stores, but they carry only a limited selection of accessories. Mass merchandisers such as Wal-Mart also carry auto accessories and there are several auto part catalogs that carry accessories, but none that carry as many products as AutoFun. The store also had stiff competition from stereo retailers that offered a wide range of auto stereo equipment. Autofun's founders felt that the market would like to have a store that people could visit often to see what was new in the market.

Impulse items, which would include many auto accessories, need to be seen to be purchased. That's why accessories sell well in an auto parts store. People are in to buy something else and see the accessory and buy it on impulse. They wouldn't have gone to a store just to buy the accessory. You can't really base a store on impulse items, like AutoFun did.

Strong Points

1. *Prolific spending.* AutoFun's target customers were people who love their cars. It's not uncommon for AutoFun's target customers to spend several thousand dollars pin-striping their cars right after they buy them. They buy things for their cars all the time and, theoretically, they would be willing to come back to the store repeatedly to purchase more products.

2. *High margins.* Retailers don't have to discount specialty products that can't be found anywhere else. High-end products with high margins are typically a winning formula. One of AutoFun's problems was that it just couldn't find enough high-end specialty products that weren't carried by other stores.

Weak Points

1. *Ease of finding the right customer.* AutoFun sold a broad range of products, including neon lights for license plates, car stereos, bike carriers, and fancy car seat covers. The problem was that different customers bought each of these products. For example, someone who wanted neon lights for his or her license plate probably wouldn't also be interested in buying a bike rack.

2. *Too few entry points.* Although there was a demand for AutoFun's products, the fact that only a small percentage of people purchased its products and they purchased them infrequently meant that AutoFun could have only a limited number of stores in any metropolitan area. Its competitors—which included, on some products, mass merchandisers like Wal-Mart and, on other products, auto parts stores—had far more entry points.

		Desired	Excellent	Average	Poor	Compensating Tactics	
						Yes	No
GREAT CUSTOMERS							
Customer Characteristics	Number	High		✔			
	Ease of Finding	Easy			✔		
	Spending Patterns	Prolific	✔				
Customer Value to Company	$ Value of Sale	High		✔			
	Repeat Sales	Many			✔		
	Ongoing Sales Support	Low	✔				
EASY SALES							
Value to Customer	How Important	Important		✔			
	Competitive Advantage	High		✔			
	Price/Value Relationship	Low		✔			
Customer Acquisition Cost	Entry Points	Many			✔		
	Sales Support Required	Little		✔			
	Promotional Activities	Low			✔		
LONG LIFE							
Profit per Sale	Margins	High	✔				
	Up-Selling and Cross-Selling	Much			✔		
	Ongoing Product Costs	Low		✔			
Investment Required	To Enter Business	Low		✔			
	To Keep Market Share	Low		✔			
	To Stay on the Cutting Edge	Low		✔			

FIGURE 6-1. AutoFun GEL factor analysis

3. *AutoFun couldn't discover any low-cost promotional activities.* Promotional costs are typically high whenever you don't have a tightly focused target customer group. You can't develop a reliable mailing list and

Put the Odds in Your Favor

New entrepreneurs typically love their ideas and they feel that they have the ability to deal with the adversity that might lie ahead. Entrepreneurs have to realize their limitations. The people who started AutoFun had just too many obstacles, no matter how smart or dedicated or hard working they may have been. The GEL factor evaluation process is not meant to discourage people from taking their ideas out into the market-place; it's meant to help them figure out how to produce a better business concept. AutoFun's biggest problem was that it didn't appeal to just one target customer group. If they had used the GEL factor analysis, the owners might have seen the problems with their concept and decided to concentrate on just one target market.

When you do a GEL factor evaluation, you need to evaluate how you stack up against competition as you score each point. AutoFun's number of entry points was low in comparison with the number of entry points for auto parts and auto stereo stores, which were its major competitors. AutoFun's number of entry points might have been acceptable if its competitors also had a limited number of entry points.

you can't partner up with other companies that target the same customers. The result is that you have to market to a large group to find the small group of customers who may want to buy your product.

4. *Repeat sales happened infrequently.* AutoFun's products—whether a rear-mounted bike rack, a neon license plate light, or a car stereo—were purchases that people make only very occasionally. The result is that AutoFun could not count on a certain level of sales each month from repeat customer, but instead had to go out and get new customers all the time.

5. *Up-selling and cross-selling opportunities were limited.* Customers that buy neon license plates might also buy a car stereo, but probably not a bike rack or an office-in-the-car product. Customers would likely find only one or two items in the store that they would consider purchasing.

		Desired	Excellent	Average	Poor	Compensating Tactics Yes	No
GREAT CUSTOMERS							
Customer Characteristics	Number	High		✔			
	Ease of Finding	Easy		✔			
	Spending Patterns	Prolific	✔				
Customer Value to Company	$ Value of Sale	High	✔				
	Repeat Sales	Many	✔				
	Ongoing Sales Support	Low		✔			
EASY SALES							
Value to Customer	How Important	Important	✔				
	Competitive Advantage	High		✔			
	Price/Value Relationship	Low		✔			
Customer Acquisition Cost	Entry Points	Many		✔			
	Sales Support Required	Little		✔			
	Promotional Activities	Low		✔			
LONG LIFE							
Profit per Sale	Margins	High	✔				
	Up-Selling and Cross-Selling	Much		✔			
	Ongoing Product Costs	Low	✔				
Investment Required	To Enter Business	Low			✔	✔	
	To Keep Market Share	Low		✔			
	To Stay on the Cutting Edge	Low			✔		✔

FIGURE 6-2. Coach GEL factor analysis

Manufacturing Company: Coach— Meeting Customer Desires

Coach is a manufacturer of high-quality handbags that was
losing market share in the late '90s to fashion designers that

were starting to do handbags. Those companies benefited from cross-selling a handbag to customers buying some of their other fashion products.

Coach's response was to hire a top designer from Tommy Hilfiger and then create a "Lifestyle" brand by expanding its line to include a full range of designer products. Finally the company added new materials to its leather standard in the handbag line and reintroduced an old logo, C, to help demonstrate that its new line was cool. The results of the company's rejuvenation strategy were pretty cool, too. Third-quarter profits for 2001 were up 158%.

Strong Points

1. *The target customers like to spend money.* There are a significant number of people who spend lots of money to keep looking good. If a company gets the "buzz" on its side, profits will be high.

2. *The purchase is important.* Looking good matters a lot to the target customer group. That means that people will look at different products as they become available and that they are willing to switch brands for a new, better look. Also, when a purchase is important, people also look at what other people are doing, which means a current customer could encourage many other people to check out a new fashion. The importance of the purchase is also why there are so many fashion magazines that cover the new styles. Moving into a more important purchase category was a major improvement over the company's old model, where it sold only leather handbags.

3. *The dollar value of the sale is high.* High fashion certainly equals high dollars. Expanding the product line also gives the company a better chance to sell

*O*ne of the dangers of being in a business like fashion where a manufacturer is either "in fashion" or "out of fashion" is that the market is fickle and companies can't predict how customers will respond. Coach's decision to start offering more products is a response to this danger. Having a broader product line offers protection in case the market turns away from a company's main product.

more products. This just relates to consumers. Having a higher dollar value also helps Coach succeed with fewer retailers. The company can work closer with its key retailers and develop better programs to promote sales.

4. *Strong potential for repeat sales.* Customers might buy a handbag and then come back to get a dress or fashion accessory to match the handbag. Plus they might remember a designer they like when they get ready to buy a new product. This again is an improvement over the old model. The target customers might have a selection of handbags, but it won't be nearly as large as their collection of clothes.

5. *High fashion typically equals high margins.* Part of the appeal of high fashion is that it is expensive and that most people can't or won't buy it—but high profits can be made off people who do buy.

Weak Points

1. *Establishing a brand name in fashion is expensive and difficult.* The main reason for this is that there are so many fashion retailers. One compensating factor for Coach was that it had already established a brand name in fashion handbags. A compensating tactic for Coach was that it hired a "hot" designer away from Tommy Hilfiger, one of the market's leading names, to lead its new products team.

2. *Staying on the leading edge is expensive and challenging.* There's no way around the fact that staying on top is risky when you sell to a market that is based solely on desires and image and not any true functional product needs. The whims of the market swing quickly and a company's market share can drop in a big

High margins provide a second benefit; they allow Coach to give its retailers lots of support to help sell its products. Manufacturers with high margins can offer retailers upscale displays, sales catalogs, special mailing pieces, and other promotional materials to help sell their products. Companies do best when they invest part of their high margins back into marketing to build the brand and help their retailers.

hurry. The customers can choose from many businesses and competition is fierce.

Service Company: Everdream— Meeting a Big Need

> *Subscription providers* provide access to high technology and support for a monthly fee.
>
> *Application service providers (ASPs)* provide only software for a monthly fee. Customers don't have to worry about equipment or software updates or how to integrate new technology into their existing business because the provider takes care of this for them. Both types of services promote trouble-free computing as their main benefit.

Everdream provides a new service category called *subscription computing*. Everdream provides software, computers, printers, networking, and everything else a company might need in computing needs for $150 to $250 per month per user. Its target market is small to mid-size businesses that can't afford a big upfront fee for computer purchases or simply don't want to waste time configuring and setting up new programs, computers, or networks. Everdream also offers 24/7 technical support, automated online back-up, virus protection, maintenance and repair, and unlimited DSL Web access with e-mail and service guarantees. Everdream allows companies to upgrade their equipment anytime after the first 12 months for a fee. Everdream boasts that in many cases companies that have five or six users would pay more to consultants to set up their computers than they pay to actually have the equipment installed, up, and running with Everdream. The company offers its services through its own Web site and sales force but primarily relies on resellers, who are established computer solutions providers to businesses that have an existing customer base and sales force.

Strong Points

1. *A high number of potential customers.* Everdream's target customers are small to mid-size companies with a low level of computer expertise. This group includes probably over half of small to mid-size companies. An Everdream salesperson could probably drive

		Desired	Excellent	Average	Poor	Compensating Tactics	
						Yes	No
GREAT CUSTOMERS							
Customer Characteristics	Number	High	✔				
	Ease of Finding	Easy		✔			
	Spending Patterns	Prolific		✔			
Customer Value to Company	$ Value of Sale	High		✔			
	Repeat Sales	Many	✔				
	Ongoing Sales Support	Low			✔	✔	
EASY SALES							
Value to Customer	How Important	Important	✔				
	Competitive Advantage	High	✔				
	Price/Value Relationship	Low		✔			
Customer Acquisition Cost	Entry Points	Many		✔			
	Sales Support Required	Little		✔			
	Promotional Activities	Low		✔			
LONG LIFE							
Profit per Sale	Margins	High		✔			
	Up-Selling and Cross-Selling	Much	✔				
	Ongoing Product Costs	Low			✔	✔	
Investment Required	To Enter Business	Low			✔		
	To Keep Market Share	Low	✔				
	To Stay on the Cutting Edge	Low		✔			

FIGURE 6-3. Everdream GEL factor analysis

down any industrial street and find several companies interested in its services.

2. *Current technology is critical for many small businesses.* In fact, technology is becoming more and more important, especially with the emergence of online market-

SUCCESSFUL BUSINESS MODELS

> *M*any new companies with a strong business model like Everdream's seem to think people will just buy because their offer is so good. That's simply not true. Sales and distribution are always a key element in any company's success and you have to commit resources to sell your product. Everdream's alliances with solutions providers as its reseller network are another strong point in the GEL factor analysis.

places for businesses and the move by many large companies to Web-enable their technology.

3. *The company has a big advantage over the traditional route businesses take to acquire technology—buying the equipment on their own.* Most small businesses don't want or can't deal with all the complexities of today's interconnected world. Setting up so a salesperson can access in-house data while on the World Wide Web is just one of the smaller challenges. Providing a turnkey solution is an enormous advantage and Everdream has only a few competitors in the subscription market.

4. *High percentage of repeat sales because of the monthly fee.* One of the advantages of a monthly fee is that people keep buying without having to make a new purchase decision. Upgrades are completed for a low cost and increase in the monthly fee, a much easier decision to make for a business than going out and buying a new set of equipment and software and then having to figure out how to get it working.

5. *There are many opportunities for cross-selling and up-selling.* Selling new software and hardware is relatively easy: first, because Everdream's monthly fee makes the buying decision relatively pain-free and, second, because the company is constantly in contact with its customers, providing technical service.

6. *The company's distribution strategy makes it easy to keep market share.* Everdream sells through solutions-based resellers, which like selling the product because it gives them another tool to use when selling small businesses. There are many of these firms in the market, they have established good reputations, and they have a customer base already in place.

86 / CHAPTER 6

Weak Points

1. *High ongoing sales support.* Everdream's customers are facing a rapidly changing technology world and they will have lots of questions for Everdream about what to do next. Everdream accepted this cost and simply built the costs of sales support into its monthly fee. The upside of the sales support is that it allows Everdream many opportunities for up-selling and cross-selling.

2. *High ongoing product costs.* One reason that Everdream's service is interesting to its customers is that the cost of upgrading technology is high. The cost is also high for Everdream. Everdream can mitigate this risk by leasing equipment and it is able to cover the lease costs in its monthly fee. The costs are a concern, though, if business turns down and those costs could put the company in jeopardy if Everdream is caught holding excess inventory.

3. *High cost of entering the business.* This is good news and bad news. The bad news is that high costs make it challenging for Everdream to build up a nationwide network of resellers. The good news is that if Everdream, as one of the earliest companies in the market, can gain strong initial market share, the high cost of entering will make it difficult for competitors to enter the market.

Small Business: American Wildlife Art Galleries—Drawing Customers

The popularity of wildlife art has been increasing over the last 10 years, with works by major artists regularly selling for anywhere from $20,000 to $50,000. The American Wildlife Art Galleries originally sold a variety of artists, but

> *People devoted to a hobby, avocation, or interest are always an ideal customer group. They will look for a business in odd places and visit frequently a business devoted to their interest. Best of all, they are willing to spend money on their interest. The only question for a small business is whether or not there are enough devoted people in the area to support their business.*

when a new owner took over, he focused on the wildlife art of Les C. Kouba, one of the founders of the wildlife art genre, who died in 1998. To bring the prices down to a level that was more affordable to most people, the store started reproducing the paintings using a process that prints the pictures onto canvas. The owner limits the reproductions to 750 to 1000 of each painting. The reproductions sell for about $600 each. The owner also produces prints of the paintings that range in price from $30 for a small-size print to more than a $100 for a full-size print.

In addition, the store sells T-shirts, playing cards, plaques, and other products based on Kouba's work. Since Kouba produced thousands of paintings, the store has an unlimited number of potential pictures to work with. The gallery is the ninth floor of an office building in downtown Minneapolis, a location somewhat out of the way for some, and operates with two employees. The business is a success because the gallery appeals to people who love wildlife art but aren't in a position to pay the high prices of original work.

Strong Points

1. *Easy to find customers.* Wildlife art enthusiasts can be found through hunting and wildlife art magazines and through art shows and exhibits that concentrate on wildlife art. The store didn't need to run an expensive ad or promotional campaign to the general public.
2. *Customers enjoy buying wildlife art.* People who enjoy wildlife art are willing to buy it, especially when it is at an affordable price.
3. *Prices of prints and reproductions are a more affordable option.* Although there are some prints and reproductions of wildlife art available, most galleries concen-

		Desired	Excellent	Average	Poor	Compensating Tactics	
						Yes	No
GREAT CUSTOMERS							
Customer Characteristics	Number	High		✔			
	Ease of Finding	Easy	✔				
	Spending Patterns	Prolific	✔				
Customer Value to Company	$ Value of Sale	High	✔				
	Repeat Sales	Many	✔				
	Ongoing Sales Support	Low	✔				
EASY SALES							
Value to Customer	How Important	Important	✔				
	Competitive Advantage	High	✔				
	Price/Value Relationship	Low		✔			
Customer Acquisition Cost	Entry Points	Many			✔	✔	
	Sales Support Required	Little		✔			
	Promotional Activities	Low		✔			
LONG LIFE							
Profit per Sale	Margins	High	✔				
	Up-Selling and Cross-Selling	Much	✔				
	Ongoing Product Costs	Low		✔			
Investment Required	To Enter Business	Low			✔	✔	
	To Keep Market Share	Low		✔			
	To Stay on the Cutting Edge	Low	✔				

FIGURE 6-4. American Wildlife Art Galleries GEL factor analysis

trate on selling the more expensive originals or prints by lesser-known artists. The gallery had a big advantage in its Minneapolis location, since Les Kouba was a Minnesota artist.

*K*ouba was a Minnesota artist who also happened to have a nationwide reputation. Often businesses try to prosper from a local angle, such as a shop of Colorado merchandise. Those stores do well with tourists, provided that tourists can find them, but often local people won't shop there. A local connection alone is not enough; the merchandise still has to succeed on its own merits.

4. *Dollar value for each sale is significant.* The lowest-price art in the store was small prints for $30 to $50. These still amount to a significant sale. Some people purchased accessories only, but those sales still easily exceeded $10.

5. *Wildlife art devotees buy art on a regular basis.* One of the positive points of serving a market where people indulge their hobbies or avocations is that people keep on buying and expanding their collections. This repeat business also generated word-of-mouth advertising, since each wildlife art enthusiast likely knows four or five others.

6. *Very little ongoing sales support is required.* One of the nice things about selling art is that it doesn't require ongoing training, interfacing, or support. Once it is sold, people hang it on a wall and pretty much nothing can go wrong.

7. *Margins are relatively high.* High-quality artwork typically is sold at a margin of at least 50%, sometimes much higher. The question about quality artwork is not how much money is made per sale, but rather how many sales can be made.

8. *There are many up-selling and cross-selling opportunities.* One of the great features of this business concept is that wildlife art enthusiasts tend to prefer the art of a select number of people. So, if they buy one item, there's a chance they will buy another.

9. *The store will have a relatively easy time staying on the cutting edge.* Kouba created thousands of works of art and he passed away in 1998; people tend to appreciate an artist more the longer he or she is in the public eye. The store just needs to keep coming up with prints from different pictures, something it should be able to do without much trouble.

Weak Points

1. *There is only one entry point—a store.* And the store is in an unusual retail location. The mitigating factor is that the owner has a distinctive strategy and product line that has very strong appeal for his target customer group.
2. *Acquiring original paintings can be difficult and expensive.* The store was able to overcome this problem because the original shop owner was the nephew of Les Kouba. He was able to acquire a collection of original paintings from family and friends to launch the shop.

Small Business: Creative Indoor Billboards—Signs of Success

This firm from Sacramento, California sells those billboards you find in restrooms in restaurants, sports bars, nightclubs, sports arenas, and other popular venues. The company is somewhat successful, with billboards in 150 locations. The ads cost anywhere from $100 to $2,000 per month, depending on the number of locations an advertiser takes, with the average customer paying about $400 per month. Monthly sales total about $50,000. Creative Indoor Billboards is offering access to a target customer group, young adults usually less than 35 who frequent nightclubs and bars. This target customer group is somewhat hard to promote to using traditional means because they don't have trade shows, magazines, or other venues that they attend, read, or go to regularly and, as a result, there are few really attractive advertising alternatives. They also don't qualify as steady TV viewers, either of cable shows or of local programs.

Creative Indoor Billboards' target customers are not the young adults, but rather the advertisers that are trying to

Retailers really have two entry points to worry about: first, how easy it is to find the store and, second, how many price points the store has. A wide variety of price points offers opportunities for every visitor to at least buy something. The store meets this second criterion with T-shirts, mugs, and other lower-cost accessories that people can buy that reflect their interest in wildlife art.

reach those young adults. The company finds its customers either because they see an ad in the restroom and call for more information or by searching ads in magazines, ads at movie theatres, direct mail pieces, and other advertising from companies trying to reach the young adult market.

Strong Points

1. *Customers should be easy to find.* Creative Indoor Billboards' customers are people who try to reach young adults. They can find those people by simply observing where companies trying to reach those target customers, advertise, or promote their business.

2. *Companies need new, innovative ways to find customers.* The advertisers' target customers, young adults, can be difficult to reach simply because they are active and may not read magazines or newspapers or even watch the same shows repeatedly. That results in the advertisers always being interested in new cost-effective ways of reaching customers. They are willing to try new techniques because it's difficult for them to reach their customers.

Weak Points

1. *Lots of sales effort is required to make sales.* People are overwhelmed by the amount of advertising and information overload that they receive. As a result, ads are no longer as effective. This is exactly why Creative Indoor Billboards' customers are looking for new ways to reach customers. It is also the reason that it requires a lot of sales effort to sell each ad.

2. *Lots of ongoing sales effort is required to keep customers buying.* One of the problems marketers have with advertising is that it might take six months to see any results; and

> **High average sale** relates the sales value to the amount of sales effort required. It's a subjective term. For a retailer, $40 to $50 is a threshold for a high average sale. A company that sends local salespeople into the field might feel $10,000 is a high average sale. When salespeople travel, a starting figure for a high average sale is $20,000. If multiple sales calls are required, the high average sales number climbs even higher.

		Desired	Excellent	Average	Poor	Compensating Tactics Yes	No
GREAT CUSTOMERS							
Customer Characteristics	Number	High		✔			
	Ease of Finding	Easy	✔				
	Spending Patterns	Prolific		✔			
Customer Value to Company	$ Value of Sale	High		✔			
	Repeat Sales	Many		✔			
	Ongoing Sales Support	Low			✔		
EASY SALES							
Value to Customer	How Important	Important	✔				
	Competitive Advantage	High		✔			
	Price/Value Relationship	Low		✔			
Customer Acquisition Cost	Entry Points	Many		✔			
	Sales Support Required	Little			✔		
	Promotional Activities	Low		✔			
LONG LIFE							
Profit per Sale	Margins	High		✔			
	Up-Selling and Cross-Selling	Much		✔			
	Ongoing Product Costs	Low		✔			
Investment Required	To Enter Business	Low		✔			
	To Keep Market Share	Low		✔			
	To Stay on the Cutting Edge	Low		✔			

FIGURE 6-5. Creative Indoor Billboards GEL factor analysis

then, even when results are obtained, they are difficult to measure. For example, four people who join a health club might mention that they saw an ad in a restaurant, but the ad might have influenced many other new members. Advertising salespeople have to keep in constant touch with their customers or they will find that customers will get discouraged and drop their ad.

Small Business: Terri's Consign and Design Furnishings—Value and Prices

The first store in this chain opened in Arizona in 1979 and now there are nine stores in the Phoenix area. Thrift stores and consignment shops are common, but Terri's does it with a twist. It offers only high- to very high-end furniture. It also supplements its merchandise with new overstock from major furniture manufacturers and stores that go out of business. The focus of the stores is offering distinctive merchandise that will make a home décor sizzle. Consignment merchandise is easy to obtain if the stores are located in upscale neighborhoods. The furniture typically has little wear and it offers a welcome addition to the homes of many middle-income families who want to have furnishings that can make a fashion statement.

Strong Points

1. *Customers are easy to find.* People with high, but not super high incomes who want upscale home furnishings can be found by buying a list of home décor magazines targeted at interior designers, getting the names of people who visit the upscale furniture marts that cater to interior designers, or using customer lists at upscale restaurants or gift shops. One of the other big advantages Terri's had was a lot of word-of-mouth advertising. People desiring a designer look often desire it because they like to entertain. Their friends probably also like to entertain and, as a result, just might be stopping at Terri's in the future.

One of the reasons for Terri's success is she realizes her business depends on having merchandise that brings people back. So her stores are in upscale neighborhoods where it's easier to get the consignment goods she is looking for. It would have been a mistake to locate the store where the customers live, as it would be harder to find consignment goods. Consider all aspects of your business before making a decision on where to locate.

		Desired	Excellent	Average	Poor	Compensating Tactics	
						Yes	No
GREAT CUSTOMERS							
Customer Characteristics	Number	High		✔			
	Ease of Finding	Easy	✔				
	Spending Patterns	Prolific		✔			
Customer Value to Company	$ Value of Sale	High		✔			
	Repeat Sales	Many		✔			
	Ongoing Sales Support	Low		✔			
EASY SALES							
Value to Customer	How Important	Important	✔				
	Competitive Advantage	High	✔				
	Price/Value Relationship	Low	✔				
Customer Acquisition Cost	Entry Points	Many		✔			
	Sales Support Required	Little		✔			
	Promotional Activities	Low		✔			
LONG LIFE							
Profit per Sale	Margins	High			✔	✔	
	Up-Selling and Cross-Selling	Much	✔				
	Ongoing Product Costs	Low			✔		
Investment Required	To Enter Business	Low		✔			
	To Keep Market Share	Low		✔			
	To Stay on the Cutting Edge	Low		✔			

FIGURE 6-6. Terri's Consign and Design Furnishings GEL factor analysis

2. *The purchase of upscale furniture is important.* Terri's targets customers who want an upscale room décor on a modest budget. Having that designer look and feel to a room is an important lifestyle choice for Terri's cus-

tomers and they are willing to go far out of their way to get the merchandise they want.

3. *The store has a competitive price advantage over high-end stores and a competitive product advantage over stores with similar prices.* Terri's is in an enviable position of having an advantage over both upscale stores, due to price, and mid-priced stores, due to the quality and look of the furniture she carries.

4. *The price/value relationship is excellent.* Terri's target customers are people who want designer furniture but can't afford it. Her product has the best value for the money of any store selling high-end furniture and it's the only way for some customers to acquire the furniture they really want.

5. *There are many opportunities for up-selling or cross-selling.* One of the great things about selling furniture is that people also need lots of accessories to make the room look complete. Those accessories are a great tool for increasing the dollar value of every customer sale.

Weak Points

1. *Margins are lower than for most retail stores.* Consignment shops might get a 20% or 25% commission, versus a margin of 50% or higher at most furniture stores. Of course, Terri's doesn't have to buy the furniture, which keeps her costs down. But Terri still has all the other expenses associated with selling a product, such as marketing, sales and administrative costs like bookkeeping, legal fees, and license costs.

2. *The cost of acquiring merchandise can be high.* Terri's depends on consistently having new consignment furniture in stock. The store needs an active campaign to acquire that stock. Terri's will also have to

> *A*ccessories sell well because they complement the original purchase. Often businesses make the mistake of taking accessories lightly and not always making sure the merchandise complements the main product line. That mistake not only loses sales the company could have made, but also probably sticks the business with unwanted inventory. Choose your accessories just as carefully as you choose your principal products.

Why Margins Count

Abusiness with a 40% margin pays $60 to acquire or make goods that it sells for $100. The margin number is before sales and marketing, administration, and other costs are taken out to determine an actual profit percentage for a business. If a company has a 40% margin, it generates $40 in profit for a $100 sale. At a 30% margin, the company has to sell $133 to generate that same $40 in profit. That's a 33% increase in sales. What makes the situation even more unfavorable for the low-margin business is that sales and marketing costs typically run as a percentage of sales. I've listed below what happens to the margins after sales and marketing costs are taken out. Company A has a 40% margin and Company B has a 30% margin.

	Company A	Company B
Sales	$100	$133
Margin	40	40
Sales and Marketing Costs (15% of sales)	15	20
Margin after Sales and Marketing	25	20

The low-margin company not only has to sell more products but it typically still makes less money. Don't buy into the theory that you can accept making less money per product and then make up for the lower margin by selling more products. A company with a strong business concept always has a strong margin position. The only viable long-term tactic for having lower prices is to have lower costs.

spend marketing dollars to promote her store to the people who will eventually buy her merchandise.

Internet Business: Webvan Group— Online Grocer

Webvan of San Francisco, launched in 1999, was one of the originators of the online grocery concept, where people order groceries online and have them delivered to their homes. The company was able to sign up 750,000 customers in its target markets of San Francisco, Los Angeles, Orange County (CA), San Diego, Seattle, Chicago, and Portland. The company burned through $830 million and closed in the summer of 2001 without ever turning a profit. Webvan failed despite having a 46% share and sales of $77 million in the first quarter of 2001. It failed because it lost $218 million in that same quarter.

Webvan's problem was that it targeted too many customers. Rather than concentrate on customers who were willing to pay the $10 to $15 (if not more) it cost to deliver groceries, the company wanted a bigger market, people who wanted groceries delivered without paying a delivery charge. This was dangerous because it had to match prices with grocery stores, which are traditionally a very low-margin business. There was no way that Webvan could afford to deliver products for free and still charge the same price as grocery stores and make money. Webvan needed to charge for the convenience of delivery. Unfortunately, Webvan placed a premium on the number of customers it acquired, a strategy that dictated that Webvan not charge. The resulting business collapse was inevitable, because its business concept was flawed. The only way for Webvan to succeed was to be able to sell other, higher-margin products to the same customers. Even that strategy might not have overcome the drawback of losing $10 to $15 per customer every time the company delivered groceries.

Strong Points

1. *Everybody buys groceries—and many of those people dislike grocery shopping.* Working people come home tired and don't particularly care to go shopping in a crowded grocery store. But they need to eat. The number of potential customers is very high, possibly

One of the comments I commonly hear from failed businesses is that they ran out of money. And that certainly can be a problem. But sometimes before struggling businesses go out to raise more money, they should first make sure they have a business concept that has a chance to produce profits. You'll never have enough money to successfully launch a bad business idea.

		Desired	Excellent	Average	Poor	Compensating Tactics	
						Yes	No
GREAT CUSTOMERS							
Customer Characteristics	Number	High	✔				
	Ease of Finding	Easy	✔				
	Spending Patterns	Prolific		✔			
Customer Value to Company	$ Value of Sale	High		✔			
	Repeat Sales	Many	✔				
	Ongoing Sales Support	Low		✔			
EASY SALES							
Value to Customer	How Important	Important		✔			
	Competitive Advantage	High	✔				
	Price/Value Relationship	Low	✔				
Customer Acquisition Cost	Entry Points	Many		✔			
	Sales Support Required	Little		✔			
	Promotional Activities	Low		✔			
LONG LIFE							
Profit per Sale	Margins	High			✔		
	Up-Selling and Cross-Selling	Much		✔			
	Ongoing Product Costs	Low		✔	✔		
Investment Required	To Enter Business	Low			✔		
	To Keep Market Share	Low			✔		
	To Stay on the Cutting Edge	Low		✔			

FIGURE 6-7. Webvan Group GEL factor analysis

25% of the total U.S. population, which is why Webvan was able to sign up 750,000 customers.

2. *People who would rather not grocery shop are easy to locate.* Webvan was able to promote its services to two-income professional families and easily locate

plenty of prospective customers.

3. *The concept of having groceries delivered at no charge or for only a small charge is a major advantage over traditional grocery stores.* People who are busy aren't interested in taking one to two hours out of their day to go grocery shopping. Adding two hours of free time to a week is a big advantage to a busy professional.

4. *Repeat sales are high, as people typically buy groceries at least once a week.* People have to keep eating and they have to keep shopping. Once customers discover they enjoy the convenience of on-line shopping, they are likely to keep using Webvan's service.

Weak Points

1. *The margins on groceries are just too small to support a business without a large delivery fee.* Webvan charged a fee for delivery, but it was way below its cost. Webvan had to take an order, send a person out to fill the order, deliver the order, and finally collect the money. Owners of a grocery store just put the merchandise on the shelves.

2. *The costs to enter the business were high.* As a rule, Internet companies are less expensive to start than brick-and-mortar businesses. But for Webvan, just the opposite was true. The company needed a warehouse in each market, an order entry system capable of handling a large number of orders, people to fill the orders, delivery drivers, and delivery vans. That all amounts to a huge cost to enter the market.

3. *Costs to keep market share are high.* One of the difficult aspects of an Internet business is that its success heavily depends on customer awareness of the site. That means that a successful business can be copied by a

Many entrepreneurs dismiss cost-based pricing in favor of market-based pricing. But cost-based pricing has its place. When Webvan started, the owners should have determined what fee they needed to collect for each delivery and then determined what customer group would have been willing to pay that price. That is the customer group, then, that Webvan should have targeted.

larger, well-funded company that will take business away from the company with the business idea. To keep market share, an Internet company has to be prepared to keep spending money on customer awareness.

Chat-Based Portal: Yack Media Services—Turning Words into Profits

EBay has shown the way to Internet success: bring people back to your site over and over again. Yack Media Services of New York City has an Internet site, Yack, that has achieved the same result with a different concept, an Internet guide to chat rooms and Internet programming. Yack was started in 1996 to make it easy for people to find the type of chat rooms they were looking for. It primarily focused on sites teenagers and young adults would be interested in, especially sports, music, and movies. Yack added something that was at the time an innovation—editorial comment about the sites, which ones were best, and a comment about the focus of the top sites. The goal was to help people get through the clutter on the Web. It has since added guides to all Internet programming and it updates all of the guides several times a day.

Yack attracts the people to the site every day, especially ones who use the Internet frequently. This allows the company to sell ad space and develop media programs that are ideal for people trying to reach the young, hip, computer-savvy market. Yack also uses its technology to provide products and services to build other portal sites to ISPs, broadband providers, and destination sites.

What Yack has done is, first, create a site that attracts lots of people that advertisers want to reach all the time and, second, create a division to sell its leading-edge technology that made portal site development possible. These are actually two business models—and both work great. For portal site advertising, Yack's customers are the advertisers trying to reach its target customer group of teenagers and young adults and providers of high-bandwidth technology for the Internet that want Yack's products and services.

> *Yack pays a high cost for technology development to stay on top. Yack can't really reduce this cost and expect to succeed, but what it does instead is figure out how to use its technology to generate two revenue streams, one on the portal itself and the other selling its technology products and services. This is a smart strategy, as it keeps Yack ahead of competition in both business models.*

Strong Points

1. *Finding advertisers for Yack's portal site is relatively easy.* Once Yack developed a base of people coming to its site, advertisers started to approach it. If that had not happened, Yack would have been able to look for advertisers in magazines, on TV shows, and at other events that cater to teenagers and young adults.

2. *Advertisers need to reach potential customers in order to stay in business.* Their success depends on effectively reaching their targeted market and they're willing to try Yack.

3. *Yack's popularity with its target customer group and the number of times people visit its sites give it a big competitive advantage.* Advertisers care about the number of exposures they get to their key customers and the number of clicks over to their sites. 60% of Yack's visitors click on ads and are an ideal target for many advertisers.

4. *Yack is successful in keeping advertisers.* Yack has repeat customers because its ads produce results. It's lost some dot-com customers because they went out of business, but for the most part it's kept its customer base.

Weak Points

1. *The costs of updating the site two to three times a day are high.* This requires staff, time, and a steady revenue

		Desired	Excellent	Average	Poor	Compensating Tactics	
						Yes	No
GREAT CUSTOMERS							
Customer Characteristics	Number	High		✔			
	Ease of Finding	Easy	✔				
	Spending Patterns	Prolific		✔			
Customer Value to Company	$ Value of Sale	High		✔			
	Repeat Sales	Many	✔				
	Ongoing Sales Support	Low		✔			
EASY SALES							
Value to Customer	How Important	Important	✔				
	Competitive Advantage	High	✔				
	Price/Value Relationship	Low		✔			
Customer Acquisition Cost	Entry Points	Many		✔			
	Sales Support Required	Little		✔			
	Promotional Activities	Low		✔			
LONG LIFE							
Profit per Sale	Margins	High		✔			
	Up-Selling and Cross-Selling	Much		✔			
	Ongoing Product Costs	Low			✔	✔	
Investment Required	To Enter Business	Low			✔	✔	
	To Keep Market Share	Low			✔	✔	
	To Stay on the Cutting Edge	Low			✔	✔	

FIGURE 6-8. Yack Media Services GEL factor analysis

stream from advertisers. Yack has many chat and Internet programming categories to spread out the costs of programmers.

2. *The cost of getting into the business is very high today.* But

that wasn't the case when Yack started out. The founders started in 1996 on their own as a part-time venture and they built awareness of their site before dot-com fever swept the land. To duplicate's Yack's position today would be expensive.

3. *Keeping market share against well-heeled competitors is costly.* In 2003 this is not a problem, as new competitors aren't getting funding. But that could change in the future. Yack minimizes the expense of maintaining and improving its site constantly by selling its technological improvements to other companies as products or services.

4. *Costs are high to stay on the cutting edge.* This is the same situation as with the costs of keeping market share. The costs are high but the company mitigates the cost by selling their developments to other companies.

Investment Advice: CyberInvest.com— Information Organized

There is nothing investors like more than more information. Right? Well, maybe not. There are just far too many sites on the Web where people can find investment advice. CyberInvest.com of San Diego, California thinks it has a solution. The free site offers 20 investing guides that provide comparisons of hundreds of the best investing resources on the Web with links to each site. The site organizes tools and resources by function, so visitors can find the best sites for online brokers, stock research, mutual funds, and global investing. The site is a home-based business that invested over $400,000 to launch the site. CyberInvest.com earns revenue from advertising and sponsorships from investment oriented advertisers. The company also earns revenues from partners with companies like Amazon.com,

One of the big problems in the dot-com/dot-bomb era was that companies had to be first with the biggest sites. Amazon and eBay are examples of companies that dominate a market. But they started small and tested their model before growing too fast. Spending wildly to be the first has proven to be disastrous for most companies. Test your business idea first; buy market share only once you know the concept works.

Beyond.com, and The Electric Newsstand, that offer investor resources through the site. CyberInvest.com has a PR program and the company has been mentioned in *Barron's*, *Money Magazine's Guide to Investing*, *Home PC*, and the *San Francisco Examiner*. CyberInvest.com target customers are the advertisers and sponsors on the site.

Strong Points

1. *The in-depth information, continuously updated, gives CyberInvest.com a competitive advantage in that it attracts new investors looking for help.* This is a key target customer group for potential advertisers that are looking to expand their customer base. The site attracts visitors because of its publicity and because it has achieved a four-star rating from the American Association of Individual Investors. The site has another advantage in that it's not owned by an investment house or a financial magazine, so advertisers don't have to worry about competing for business with the site's owner.

Weak Points

1. *The site has few entry points.* Entry points for a Web site include links from other sites and promotional activities that make people aware that the site exists. There are some links to the CyberInvest.com site, but not many, and the company simply can't afford an extensive promotional or advertising campaign to bring its name to the public.

2. *Sales support is required for each advertiser.* Advertising is always a tough sale, because there are so many advertising opportunities available to people and because most advertising vehicles have difficulty

> When judging their product's sales potential, entrepreneurs often only consider their product's strengths. That's not enough to gauge possible success. You have to consider also the customers' history with new ventures selling the same benefit. Investment companies have had hundreds if not thousands of sales pitches for new potential advertising venues. Most of those venues have failed and that history will make potential advertisers skeptical of another new offer.

		Desired	Excellent	Average	Poor	Compensating Tactics	
						Yes	No
GREAT CUSTOMERS							
Customer Characteristics	Number	High		✔			
	Ease of Finding	Easy		✔			
	Spending Patterns	Prolific		✔			
Customer Value to Company	$ Value of Sale	High		✔			
	Repeat Sales	Many		✔			
	Ongoing Sales Support	Low			✔		
EASY SALES							
Value to Customer	How Important	Important		✔			
	Competitive Advantage	High	✔				
	Price/Value Relationship	Low		✔			
Customer Acquisition Cost	Entry Points	Many			✔		
	Sales Support Required	Little			✔		
	Promotional Activities	Low			✔		
LONG LIFE							
Profit per Sale	Margins	High		✔			
	Up-Selling and Cross-Selling	Much		✔			
	Ongoing Product Costs	Low			✔		
Investment Required	To Enter Business	Low			✔		
	To Keep Market Share	Low			✔		
	To Stay on the Cutting Edge	Low		✔			

FIGURE 6-9. CyberInvest.com GEL factor analysis

proving that advertising with them pays off. A home-based business typically flounders when the amount of support to make each sale is high.

3. *The site needs a constant stream of promotional activities to attract new visitors.* The good news for the site is

that access to new investors is important to advertisers. The bad news is that the site has to find those new investors with an extensive promotional campaign all the time. Again, this is tough for a home-based business. Typically a home-based business will do better with a site that appeals to a small number of enthusiasts who will visit the site all the time, in part because there are few other sites serving them.

4. *The company needs to constantly spend money updating and improving its site.* Keeping the site up to date, creating new links to other sites, and continuing to monitor the investment advice from a variety of sites are time-consuming and expensive. Without constant updates, the site stands a good chance of losing its appeal to the media, which will greatly reduce the effectiveness of a PR campaign.

5. *The costs are high both for entering the business and for keeping market share.* $400,000 sounds like a big investment for a home-based business, but that's small potatoes compared with what many people are spending to develop a portal or magnet site that will attract visitors. Investment sites spend lots of money and Cyber-Invest.com will have to do the same if it wants to be considered a player in the Internet investment world.

Rules Stay the Same

Internet sites have soared like eagles and then dived like hawks. The biggest problem was that companies felt that somehow the Internet had a new set of business rules because of its promise. But that hasn't proven to be the case.

Bringing people to a Web site has proven, if anything, to be more expensive than promoting a brick-

and-mortar business. Selling a product has proven to be difficult, as people are often happier buying in a store where they can see what a product is like. And the cost of stocking and shipping products has ended up being just as costly as running a store. The only sites that have proven successful are those that get repeat visitors all the time, sell information, or ship products through other companies. EBay is a great example of the perfect Internet business: it doesn't have inventory, it has lots of repeat visitors, and it has lots of people selling products.

What went wrong with the initial expectations of Internet business? The most obvious problem is that the costs of doing business on the Internet are far higher than people expected. I believe the primary problem is that people don't have confidence in what they buy when they can't see, feel, and touch it. They also like personal contact and like to be sold. Neither happens on the Internet. But that's not to count the Internet out. It's a great supplement for brick-and-mortar and catalog businesses and it has unlimited opportunities in business-to-business commerce.

The other type of business where the Internet excels is one that offers specialized merchandise that is highly valued by a few people. Examples might be collectors of Victorian snuffboxes, teenage boys who like obscure punk bands, or people who have created a Japanese garden in their back yards. These people can't find the products in regular retail outlets because the demand for those products is too small in any geographic area.

SECTION II
PART ONE

▲ ▲ ▲

THE BUSINESS PLAN
UNDERSTANDING THE PARTS

EXECUTING A SUCCESSFUL BUSINESS CONCEPT

PLAN FOR SUCCESS ◀

Once you have you used the GEL factor analysis to fine-tune your business, you'll likely want to put it into a plan. A plan is the most effective way to put your business concept into practice. But the hard fact is that most of the established businesses I've worked with don't have business plans unless they need to raise money. Other people I talk to who deal with both small and large businesses have discovered the same thing. If you ask business owners for their business plan, they will often tell you that there might be one around from four or five years ago. Or they might tell you they have a plan they did for the bank, but that their companies are not actually following the plan, which is one reason I've separated out the book into two sections: the GEL factor analysis and the business plan. I want every business owner to at least consider ways to upgrade his or her business concept every year.

Six Reasons

Just because people don't always do a plan doesn't mean that there aren't important reasons for doing so. Here are a few reasons why:

1. *To get financing.* No matter how successful you are currently, you'll still need to provide a business plan with a full set of financial projections to investors, banks, and even potential business partners.

2. *To communicate your company's strategy.* Employees are much more productive when they have a clear understanding of a business's objectives and strategy. You should not minimize this need for communication. In some of the companies where I've consulted, I've found there is disagreement among employees on which customers the company is targeting.

3. *As a development tool.* A business plan works out the details of how a business concept will be implemented, including the anticipation of problems that might emerge.

4. *As a resource planner.* New personnel, finances, manufacturing capacity, and inventory are just a few of a company's resources that a thoughtfully prepared business plan can specify.

5. *As a standard for evaluation.* How do investors and management decide if the company has had a good year? The business plan lays out what a company hopes to accomplish and provides a baseline for determining how well management or the company's owner has done to meet those goals. It thus is a useful way to evaluate performance.

6. *To set a budget.* Monthly revenue and expense budgets are two essential tools for companies to track and use for planning during the year. The budget or financial projections also are what investors follow closely.

Plans Can Vary

Realistically, businesses use a plan as a working document that gets modified based on changing situations and circumstances. Therefore, the major goal of the plan is not a comprehensive step-by-step action plan, but rather a statement of philosophy—why you are in business, what factors point to success, and how you plan on approaching the market to take advantage of the opportunity before you. The four key elements of any business are customers with a pronounced need or desire, a product or service to meet that need or desire, a strategy for bringing that product or service to these customers, and finally people in management with the experience to make it all work.

You don't have to follow any business plan format exactly, and you have the freedom to tell your story any way you want. The only exception to this rule is the financial section and the capitalization structure, which explain who owns how much of the company and how the ownership percentages will change when the company acquires new investors. These sections are especially important if you are raising money either from investors or from banks.

> *A business plan, no matter what its purpose, has to have a simple story underlying it that investors, employees, and bankers can understand. The story needs to explain why the business makes sense and should succeed. A great plan will give people two to three sentences that explain the entire essence of the business. I recommend you write these two or three tell-all sentences before starting the plan.*

Company Goals

One last point a business plan must make clear is an overriding goal for the company. The goal is important for investors, bankers, and, I believe, for employees of the company. In raising money from professional investors or venture capitalists, entrepreneurs typically limit their goal to rapidly gaining market share so the company can sell stock through an initial public offering.

You should also have additional business measurable goals, such as to dominate a market, to gain 10% market share, to become the preferred supplier of five major com-

> *I talk to business owners all the time who don't write a plan because they "have it all in their head." This is a big mistake. The advantage a plan has it forces you to look at opportunities, market changes, and potential strategies before those factors impact your business. Business owners who have the plan in their head typically don't react until their sales fall off, which may be too late.*

panies, to develop a market foothold in one geographic market, or to establish a partnership network that provides nationwide sales coverage. Private investors want to see fast growth and a big return on their investments.

Most businesses have more limited objectives than going public. The owners want to just develop a business that will grow to produce a steady income. For example, an engineer at a company that does a lot of machining might see that the market needs a better product to collect the mist that develops from the cutting oil. The engineer's goal might just be to develop a business with the potential of a million dollars in annual sales. The short-term goals might be to engineer the best mist collector on the market and then to sign 15 distributors to sell the product. This engineer might get money from friends, family, and business acquaintances, or through a bank or the Small Business Administration.

Other entrepreneurs start a service or retail business based upon changes in the market, the success of similar businesses, or their past job experience. These individuals typically have a goal of first positioning their businesses so they have advantages over competitors, either in location, product offerings, pricing, or service, and then of establishing a customer base capable of generating a certain income level per year.

Comprehensive but Concise

You never want to treat a business plan lightly, especially if you're trying to raise money. The way your plan is written says something about you and the company's management style. Your plan needs to be thorough and comprehensive, but at the same time it has to show that you can discern and focus on the key elements of your business.

I've found that people who really understand their business can come to the heart of the matter quickly. They don't ramble on, and they focus on the issues that the company has to address to succeed. One of the biggest mistakes entrepreneurs make, especially if they are trying to land investors, is to list too many supporting facts to make a point. I've seen plans with as many as nine or ten facts to support one point. Avoid redundancy and too many facts at all costs. Remember instead the two- to three-sentence description of your business I recommended writing at the beginning of the chapter. Communicate precisely and clearly.

P *ie charts and graphs are tools often used in plans to show simple facts like market shares. Charts can be quite useful when lots of information needs to be communicated concisely. For example, you can show the differences between your product or service and that of your competitors with a chart that shows what features each product has. The buying patterns of potential target customer groups can also be easily shown in a chart.*

THE EXECUTIVE SUMMARY

GIVING THEM THE ESSENCE ◀

The executive summary of your business plan offers a capsule view of your plan, hopefully in no more than 1,000 words. The executive summary is the most important part of the plan, for two reasons. First, it's the only part of the plan many investors will read in order to decide if they want to talk with you. Second, most people won't continue to read the plan if the executive summary doesn't catch their attention. You should have almost every sentence in the summary make a new point and you need to avoid long explanations for any one item.

What to Communicate

1. *The essence of the venture.* Business owners tend to know their business too well and assume that other people will understand it right away. This is a major mistake if you have a business that is new or out of the ordinary. My experience is that people reading a business plan summary of a new business don't understand the business concept almost 50% of the time. I recommend that you give people three sentences, of not more than 40 words, that describe your business. Ask people to read those words and explain what your business is. If they can't do that, you need to work harder on describing your business.

2. *Your unique or special opportunity.* You obviously decided to go into the particular business because something about it appealed to you. That appeal is what you want to express. Perhaps your location is special, you have access to special merchandise or technology, you have an alliance with a key person or company, or you are in a unique position to solve your customers' problems or help them meet their desires.

3. *Management's goals.* No matter who your audience is— investors, bankers, or employees—they all are concerned about just what your goals are. I've found that everyone reading the plan wants to see an ambitious goal, not necessarily in term of sales, but certainly in terms of market share. One company I worked with had a goal of achieving 1% market share after two years. That goal doesn't inspire anyone. Your market share goal could be for just one state or just one market, but be sure the goal represents a significant achievement. I've found that everyone reading a plan looks for some passion, some ambition, and some

*E*ven though the executive summary is the first part of the plan, I've found it works best to write the summary last. Most writers are a little fuzzy about exactly how the plan will come out when they start writing the plan. Their thinking crystallizes as they write, which will make it much easier to write the summary and ensure that the summary matches the points of the plan.

dedication in the business owner or management team. You'll never convince someone you have that if your goal is not at least moderately ambitious.

Format

Your summary does not have to follow this exact format, but you should be sure it covers these points.

1. *Description.* Start the section with the name of the company, what type of company it is (i.e., sole proprietorship, Subchapter S, partnership, or other), and where the company is located. People will often also state how old the business is.

2. *Concept.* In 40 words or less, state your business concept. Most plans consolidate the description and the concept into an Introduction section. State how you will make revenue, if there's any doubt possible. For example, dot-com companies might make revenue from sales, ads, links, or affiliate agreements.

3. *Customer Group.* Define your customer group by at least one and preferably two qualities. For example, young males interested in extreme sports, people interested in faux painting of their home, or people who keep koi (goldfish) in ponds in their backyards. The customer group is one of the most important points in a plan, because it's key to determining whether or not your business concept is good.

4. *Customer Need or Desire.* To succeed, a company needs a strong reason for customers to buy its product. That reason is typically based upon the customer's need or desire much more than on lower prices, better features, or better aesthetics. You want to show that customers are motivated to buy your product.

Space is the latest term used by venture capitalists and investors. It's what used to be called a "market niche." Examples of space might be top-of-the-line mountain bikes for high-end consumers, e-commerce solutions for medical companies, or software solutions for music store inventory management. To catch the full definition of a company's space, you need to list both the customer group and the product category.

5. *Market Size.* Great customers with a strong desire to buy in a big market. What could be better? Not very much. The actual size of the market is not as important as its relationship to a company's goals. I've found an idea market size is between 10% and 20% of your eventual business goals. For example, if you want to be one of the top restaurants in Northeast Cincinnati, you might want to define your geographic area to include five to 10 other top restaurants in the area. Most companies have trouble gaining more than 20% market share—competition is just too fierce. If you aim for less than 10% market share, you will have trouble being noticed in the market.

6. *Goals.* You will list sales goals and history at the end of the summary as numbers, but I feel you should state your market share goal right after market size. Clearly define your market in terms of customer group, application or market segment, and, if relevant, geographic area.

7. *Key Advantage.* The important point in the executive summary is that you have a lucrative customer group. You only have to mention briefly in the summary that you have a competitive advantage. Too often plans try to explain that advantage in detail in the summary. If people want to know more, they'll read it in a following section in the plan. The key in the summary is to list the advantage in a short phrase that's easy to remember. For example, Guitarland has twice the inventory of its competitors, XYZ's patented technology is three times as effective as the competition, and Freight Tomorrow has the most extensive fulfillment facility in the Denver area. Simple statements like this will show you are not a "me-too" company.

Business owners and marketers know their product, service, and market backwards and forwards. They often try to impress the readers of their business plan with their expertise. Unfortunately, people understand less and less of your business concept as you increase the technical content of your plan. If you are working to raise money or get a loan, concentrate on making your business easy to understand.

8. *Timing.* In some cases timing is critical, such as new retail businesses in a growing neighborhood, a new type of service business, or the introduction of a new product for a new application. If timing is critical, especially in the case of changes in the market, explain why.

9. *Management.* This is key to any successful business. You will have trouble getting money even with a great business model if you don't have a strong management team. If there are just one or two managers or if your experience is light, you need to have a team of advisors with lots of experience in your industry. I've found it worthwhile to give up equity if necessary to attract the type of managers who will make your venture grow. The most important feature in the summary is past business experience with relevant companies.

10. *Operations.* This section would mention manufacturing facilities, administration, and other business functions. This normally isn't included in the summary unless the company's operations offer it a unique advantage in the market.

11. *Sales History/Projections/Margins.* This section typically gives sales, if any, for the last two years and projections for the next three years. It's also appropriate to list the margins you expect each year. Some people will also list the income per year.

This section is often presented in whatever format shows the company in the most positive light. Income is left off if a company is losing money. Only the prior year's sales are shown if sales have not been growing. Future sales need to be realistic in the first year of the plan; after that they can grow.

Business plans tend to project the future in dramatically different ways depending on the objective. Businesses that are looking for investors often show sales doubling or even tripling every year. Investors want to see the business growing rapidly, even if to grow it has to spend all of its profits on sales and marketing activities. A business plan oriented toward getting money from a banker will be more conservative, showing profits much sooner and showing that money invested will be going toward tangible assets such as equipment and inventory.

12. *Capitalization or Financing Plan.* This section should be included anytime you are selling stock or borrowing money. If you are not borrowing or raising money, you can leave this section out.

If you're approaching investors or a bank, always start this section by stating how much money you are raising or borrowing. *Capitalization* is a statement of what a company is worth. It's calculated by multiplying the number of shares that are owned in the company by the price you're currently charging for buying shares. Investors also want to see how much of the company is being bought in the current round of funding. For capitalization, list the number of shares currently owned, the number you're trying to sell, and the total number of shares owned.

You may also be borrowing money for your business. You would want to list here the sources of the money: for example, a percentage from your resources, a percentage from vendors, and a percentage from a bank.

No one is more attuned to the Internet than the 15-to-24-year-old age group. 40% of this age group's Internet users click on ads and links and buy products off the

> *I've consulted for many companies where employees think the sales numbers in a plan are smoke and mirrors for investors. This is a dangerous situation, as investors and bankers will eventually talk with some of those employees and it won't take them long to see that employees don't believe the numbers. Before you finalize the plan, be sure your staff buys into your growth for the future.*

Internet. Every company serious about success needs a Web site. And because technology is increasing so rapidly, these Web sites need to be redesigned and maintained on a regular basis.

Sample Section—Princeton WebSolutions

Business plan author: Michael Simmons, President and CEO

Executive Summary

Company Description

Princeton WebSolutions (PWS) is a student-run e-business solutions provider with core competencies in Internet consulting and Web development. PWS specifically focuses on companies that market to the college student demographic. In 2000, PWS was rated the #1 youth-run Web development company in the nation by YoungBiz.

Opportunity

Companies are spending large sums of money to try and figure out how to market to the 70 million youth from Generation Y, people born from 1979 to 1994. Some companies have been successful, however most companies have not been, due in part to their lack of understanding of their target customers because they themselves are years and sometimes even decades removed from this generation. Enter Princeton WebSolutions All of PWS employees are college students and they know what college students want. PWS is uniquely positioned to offer clients an insider's view to reaching this target market.

The PWS strategy is to offer companies low-cost, appealing Web sites. It achieves this objective by employing college students to develop appealing content and then outsourcing the programming and Web site development to overseas programming firms. PWS is able to provide high-quality work at low prices and high margins. PWS has been able to exceed client expectations, while charging approximately 50% below the industry average, and still have profit margins of over 30%.

Products and Benefits

Princeton WebSolutions offers Internet consulting and Web development, which consists of Web design and programming.

- Internet consulting entails gathering information on the client's company, industry, market, and customer and then planning how the client can most effectively use the Internet.
- Web design includes online branding, usability engineering (creating an easily navigated Web site), and multimedia. Online branding consists of the visual look, typography, content, logo, and any other messages the Web site sends to the end user.
- Programming includes the creation of e-business and custom Web applications, such as content management, customer relationship management, and e-commerce systems.

Management

Michael Simmons, company cofounder. Sophomore at the Stern School of Business at NYU. Winner of the 2000 Young Entrepreneur of the Year Award for New York City from the Fleet Youth Entrepreneur Expo.

This plan combines information on its target customer, businesses marketing to Generation Y, and the customers' needs, effectively communicating to Generation Y, into one section called Opportunity. "Opportunity" is a positive term and more interesting than section headings like "Customer Group" and "Customer Need." Remember that your business plan is in most cases an effort to sell your company.

Business experience includes working for Operation Enterprise, the young adult division of the American Management Association.

Daniel Blank, Chief Creative Officer. Marketing major at the Stern School of business at NYU majoring in marketing. He has worked at several intern positions in the new media industry and his personal Web site can be viewed at www.daniel-blank.com.

Rishi Chhabria, Chief Business Development Officer. A junior in Finance and Marketing at the Stern School of Business, NYU. His business experience includes working for investment companies The Heartland Advisors and A.G. Edwards and he has worked part-time doing graphic design for New York University Athletics.

Richard Salem, Chief Marketing Officer. Creator of the PWS Web site and a major in Journalism and Mass Communications with a minor in Computer Science at the Stern School of Business at NYU. Business experience includes sales, field training, and sales management for Vector Marketing.

Advisory Board
PWS currently doesn't have an advisory board but will be setting one up by the end of 2001.

The Industry
No one is more attuned to the Internet than the 15-to-24-year-old age group. 40% of this age group's Internet users click on ads and links and buy products off the Internet. Every company serious about success needs a Web site. And because technology is increasing so

P WS's managers obviously have limited management experience because they're young. But they're go-getters. They're showing management maturity by proposing an advisory board. A weakness is that they don't have an office. The ideal situation for PWS would be to find a mentor who would allow PWS to use his or her office as a mailing and phone address. Investors and bankers will appreciate daily support for PWS from an experienced mentor.

rapidly, these Web sites need to be redesigned and maintained on a regular basis.

Competitive Strategy

PWS is positioning itself in the current market by focusing on providing cost-effective, guaranteed solutions and targeting a very specific market niche in which it has expertise.

Low price is a feature offered by other firms that do Web-based programming overseas. But those firms don't have the PWS advantage of also being able to deliver the content and format young adults want. That expertise, which advertisers like VW have learned to cherish, is typically only available from high-priced advertising agencies. PWS has two competitive advantages over those agencies. One is low cost: our Web development fees are typically 80% of what an advertiser might charge. The second is that PWS will work with small and midsize firms that advertising agencies typically don't target.

Goals

1. $100,00 in revenue for the year starting September 1, 2001.
2. Raise $40,000 in private investments by January 2002.
3. Duplicate the successful New York City office to other cities by January 2003.

Most new businesses set the price of stock on their first investment go-around at 50 cents to $1 per share. One of the sales points given to early investors is that they are getting in cheap, that the stock will be more expensive on future rounds of fundraising. In other words, you're saying, "Buy now because the stock is cheap." The sales price of 50 cents to a dollar reinforces that image.

Financial Summary

Year	Sales	Profit
2000	$40,015	$13,500
2001	$100,000	$35,000
2002	$400,000	$175,000
2003	$1,000,000	$450,000

Capitalization		**Percent Ownership**
Current shares	160	62.5%
Shares offered at		
$1,000 per share	60	37.5%
Total Shares:	220	100.0%

OVERVIEW

TELLING THEM WHAT YOU'RE GOING TO TELL THEM ◀

T he business plan is constantly selling the concept of a unique opportunity. The obvious place to do this is when you describe your product or service and its proprietary features. But I think a more important place to emphasize the uniqueness is in telling how the business comes together.

For example, a technology company stated in its overview that it was an offshoot of an organization that had 200 computer programmers. That implies plenty of programming power. A company that sold medical products included in its overview the story of how the product was invented by an operating room nurse and was then immediately purchased by four area hospitals. Better yet are stories of companies where the idea sat and percolated until the right management team came together. You should try to make this section of the plan a story that explains why the owners found starting a company so compelling.

The purpose of this section is to show that your business makes lots of sense and that you got into business only after careful thought and lots of research. This is the part of the plan where you show people just how seriously you approached going into business. The overview is really just a capsule view of why you went into business and what your business has done to date. If you've been in business for a while, you want this section to show how you've positioned your business in the past, what changes you've made, and how you've set the stage for your future moves.

How careful will you be running your business? Well, people can't really tell, but one of the ways they judge you is by how carefully you've moved with your company till the timeframe of your plan. Spend a little extra time in the overview to demonstrate that you are a thoughtful businessperson. I've found people's confidence in entrepreneurs is often related to how well they present the beginnings of their business.

What to Communicate

1. *That you founded this business because of a real and significant opportunity.*
2. *That you've carefully looked into this opportunity before moving ahead.* I believe it's worthwhile to include a few interviews with real customers in this section about the market opportunity.
3. *That you've assembled the people and resources and connections to move forward on this opportunity.* Even if the people are mentors or just offering advice, list the industry people who have encouraged you to move ahead.
4. *Perhaps most importantly, that you have assembled or have access to people experienced in the market and industry that you're targeting.*

Format

1. *Describe your business.* Include the following information in your plan:
   - the business structure, e.g., a sole proprietorship or partnership

- the type of business, e.g., a retail store, an Internet seller, a manufacturer, or a service company
- how you produce income—your product or service
- your target customers
- your market
- how your product is distributed
- how you make your product or provide your service

2. *Explain your company's background.* This should be a story about why you and the other founders thought this was a great business opportunity to explore or what was so intriguing about the idea that got you started. I've found over the years that most entrepreneurs have an exceptionally strong reason for going into business, something that impressed them and gave them the fire inside that they needed to get their idea to the market. You need to convey that passion or strong reason here.

3. *List any significant events that have occurred.* This is actually a part of the company's history or overview, but I like to include a special section to highlight any points I feel are particularly important. This tactic is particularly important if you want to raise money from investors, because many of them will skim the plan. A "significant events" section will typically catch their attention.

4. *Explain your company's current status.* You need to tell exactly where you are. I've found that investors and other plan readers get irritated when entrepreneurs sugar-coat the company's current status too much. If it's bad, state why it's bad—and then say why the situation has turned around. I've found that both investors and banks expect entrepreneurs to encounter troubles. It doesn't bother them as long as

> *B*usiness plans too often read like a business or market research report. But investors, banks, and even employees want to see commitment or a passion that will carry forth even when things aren't going well. Sometimes that passion is evident from the time you've invested in your business already or from past activities related to your business. Don't be afraid to express why your business is more than just a job.

> *You're obviously in business because you think you have a great business concept. Don't sell your concept short by being too conservative when talking about your future growth. People expect entrepreneurs to oversell their potential a little bit, so they'll feel you don't have a passion for your business if you're too conservative.*

the entrepreneurs deal with the problems. Hiding from the problems is the worst-case scenario.

5. *Outline your future plans for the company.* Many plans like to list a vision or a mission here, but those statements usually are idealistic and don't really offer much insight into how the company is going to evolve. In this section, you should talk about how you will grow your business from its current levels. You shouldn't worry about whether you have the money now to reach those levels, only that this is where your business could go if everything works out right. This is especially true if you need investors, who will usually look for businesses with growth rates of over 100% per year.

Sample Section—Princeton WebSolutions

Business plan author: Michael Simmons, President and CEO.

Overview

Company Description

Princeton WebSolutions (PWS) is a student-run partnership that provides Internet design and marketing solutions for midsized companies targeting college students. PWS's two product offerings are consulting services that help companies determine how they can more effectively reach college students through the Internet and Web design services. PWS sells its services to both advertising agencies and the companies directly through the personal contact from its sales staff, which at the moment also includes management.

PWS provides its consulting services through its current staff and provides the Web design services with its in-house project management team, which directs its low-cost overseas programming team. In 2000, PWS was rated the #1 youth-run Web development company in the nation by YoungBiz.

History

Michael Simmons and Calvin Newport created PWS in September 1998. The company was founded initially because the student entrepreneurs wanted to get involved in what was at that time the "red-hot" Internet market. While trying to decide exactly how to enter the market, the founders started to concentrate on how poor many of the sites were that targeted college students. The sites moved too slow and didn't offer the college students the navigating ability they wanted. Researching the market further, the founders discovered that many large consumer companies were developing new strategies for Generation Y. "We felt that left an opening serving midsize to small companies. They may have been able to get the technical expertise for their Web site, but they didn't know how to effectively reach college students. The success of bigger companies' marketing campaigns only emphasized the shortcomings of small to midsize companies."

Since the company's expertise was knowing what students wanted to see, in the first year a partnership was formed with Princeton Online, a local community Web site, to actually do the Web-based programming. In the beginning of the second year, another partnership was formed with a Web development team in India. This partnership allowed Princeton WebSolu-

The ideal situation for an entrepreneur is to have customers who know they have a need and who want to solve their need. Your plan will be much stronger here if you talk about what your customers feel or know regarding their needs, rather than talking about why you feel they will buy. Try to include firsthand information from customers about how they perceive their need.

How does a business plan make lemonade out of lemons? In this case, it was definitely a lemon that Newport left the company. To make lemonade, simply ask what would make Newport leaving a positive for the company. The answer is that he didn't fit into the company's business concept. Once you have that answer, it's not difficult to at least neutralize the impact of his departure.

tions to offer more complex and sophisticated services for a reasonable cost and allowed Newport and Simmons to focus on project managing and running the company. As more clients were serviced, the founders saw an opportunity. This opportunity was using their expertise marketing to college students to sell customers and then forming additional partnerships with other Web development teams. This also allowed Newport and Simmons to pick the development team that was best suited to each project. Since its inception in 1998, PWS has successfully worked with over 20 different Web development companies, both domestically and internationally.

Between January 2001 and June 2001, both partners spent less time on the business and focused on schoolwork, other aspects of college, and other interests. Simmons researched and began work on "The Value-Growth Manifesto," a self-development book for teens, played on the NYU varsity tennis team, and went to many self-development seminars. During this time, less work was done on the company so little revenue was created. This was due in part to the down market and the fact that Newport and Simmons were at different locations and operating on different schedules. In June 2001, Newport officially left Princeton WebSolutions to pursue technical aspects of computer science. Simmons decided that PWS was basically a marketing company, selling the concept of youth-oriented Web pages by youths, and to look for more marketing-oriented partners.

Significant Events

PWS was reenergized in 2000 with the addition of

three management team members that were just as enthused about PWS's business potential as the founders. The most important was Richard Salem, who helped crystallize the company's Generation Y marketing strategy and developed the PWS Web site. Before Salem came on board, the company didn't have money to fully develop its own site, which limited PWS sales efforts. With a site up, PWS attracted two more employees, including one with experience in several advertising agencies, giving PWS the human resources it needs to move the business ahead.

Current Status

The company is a virtual company, with its managers communicating primarily through e-mail when not in school. The company has been developing its marketing targets and has created a list of 40 key target accounts to add to its current small sales base. The sales responsibility for those accounts has split among its managers. Initial work has begun contacting the target customers and revenues are expected in the fourth quarter of 2001. Initially, PWS is approaching each of its target companies with an offer about doing a short research report with college students to see how they react to the company's site. The second step is to offer consulting help to redesign the client's site with marketing and technical assistance. PWS expects to get eight initial consulting contracts for Web site evaluations prior to the end of 2000. The company has partnerships in place with four Web development firms in case a Web development contract is awarded.

Better yield, better pricing, and better quality. This has a perfect sound for most readers. One of the tactics you learn in writing is that, for some reason, people respond positively to groups of threes. Three—three benefits, three words in alliteration, or three facts—seems to have a much better impact than two or four. The rule of three also prevents you from listing way too many facts in your plan.

Future Plans

PWS's mission is to be the leading providing of e-business solutions to large companies that target college students in the world. The company's plan to do this is to develop sales franchises throughout the country, promoted primarily by students, and then handle the technical development partnerships for the franchises to create college-student-friendly Web pages.

PWS's strongest sales point is that it knows what college students want, because the managers are college students. At the same time, college students want experience in an entrepreneurial environment. PWS wants to meld those two together with its franchises located at colleges in major metropolitan areas. What PWS plans to offer to entrepreneurs is a successful model: first, helping clients research how college students respond; second, helping clients recast their Web page marketing tools; and finally, being able to offer, through domestic and offshore partnerships, low-cost Web development. Using students as the sales force takes advantage not only of the students' enthusiasm and energy but also helps PWS reinforce its benefit statement.

Long term, PWS will make money from franchise fees, including upfront and ongoing percentage fees, from market research it conducts for its franchises' clients, and from arranging for low-cost Web development services. Short term, PWS will be working to prove its model works effectively in the New York City area so that it can create and sell its franchise model.

TARGET CUSTOMERS AND MARKETS

FINDING WHO YOU CAN DO BUSINESS WITH ◀

Many companies put a company description after the executive summary. My experience is that people either don't read or don't understand the company description if it is placed here. Instead, I prefer to place the description in the "Company Operations" section, which comes after you explain your customers, products, markets, competitive advantages, and marketing strategy. That's when the readers of your plan have the information they need to understand your business description.

This section of the plan should explain the customer group you're targeting and the market that you are focusing on. The customers and market are tied together. For example, Amazon's target customers are people who buy lots of books and its market is Internet book sales. Amazon's customers may buy from other booksellers, such as direct sales or retail stores, and those markets compete with the Internet book market, but Amazon isn't in those markets.

What to Communicate

1. *You have identified and can narrowly define a target customer group.* One of the words you hear in this context all the time, from investors and bankers, is *focus*. You want to show not only that you know your target customer group but also that you have built your business around their needs and desires.

2. The target customer group is large, easy to find, and free spending. Of course, most businesses don't have such a dream customer group, but you want to show that your customer group is one that will be receptive to your product.

3. *Customers have a need or desire that you will fulfill.* You want to show that you offer something that the customers need or desire and you want to explain why they need or desire it.

4. *The market is well-defined, easy to penetrate, not overcrowded, and reached through defined distribution channels.* You'll find that most investors and banks steer away from new market channels until they are proven. The Internet, for example, existed for about 10 years before it became the "hot new market." New markets are full of question marks and danger.

Format

I recommend you have three main headings in this section, Customers, Opportunity, and Market. You may want to add a special section if it enhances your plan and possible business success. You want to be sure to cover the following points.

1. *Customers—characteristics.* Describe the group and some of their characteristics as they are relevant to your business. Don't get carried away in this part:

> *You need to be specific when defining a customer group. You don't want to simply state that you sell products to "manufacturers." It's better to put "manufacturers with machine shops," better yet to add "that have a lot of CNC milling machines," and even better to add "that machine stainless steel." The more narrowly you define your customer group, the easier it is to determine the customers' needs.*

just give enough information to let the reader understand who the customer is.

2. *Customers—numbers.* If possible, give the number of
    customers or otherwise show that there are enough
    customers to support your business.

3. *Customers—facts.* You want to show that you've
    researched your customers and understand them
    well. You don't want to burden the reader with facts
    here, but you must show more than just library
    research. You need to demonstrate an "industry
    insider" understanding of the customer. Present facts
    here, though, only if they're relevant to your business
    concept.

4. *Customers—how they can be reached or identified.*
    Include this information if it's not obvious how you'll
    find customers. In many cases, businesses don't have
    trouble identifying customers and you don't need to
    include this part. But in other cases, identifying them
    can be quite a problem. For example, how do you
    identify companies that are in the market for an e-
    procurement system?

5. *Opportunity—what is the need or desire?* You need to
    explain why customers are going to be motivated to
    buy your product. The answer is never that your
    product or service is great with tons of benefits. The
    answer is always that the customers are buying for
    their agenda—whether emotion, ego, functionality, or
    desire to please others.

6. *Opportunity—why the need or desire is important.* How
    can you prove that something is important? I've
    found that the best way is to demonstrate what people
    are doing already to meet this need or desire. What
    other products or services are they buying or what
    steps are they taking in their life to meet this need or

> *C*ustomers and their behavior are not easy to understand. I've found that one of the major flaws in many businesses is that the company doesn't really understand their customer. The best way to demonstrate you know the customer is if you and some of your managers are members of the customer group or if one of your managers has success-fully sold to the group at anoth-er company.

satisfy this desire? The greater the effort they make, the more important the need or desire is to them.

7. *Opportunity—the choices.* You should list other ways people could or are meeting this need or desire. You want to list direct competitors, if you have any, or indirect competitors, which are different products people buy to meet the same need. For example, wallpaper or regular painting would be substitutes or indirect competitors for faux painting.

8. *Opportunity—the reason other choices aren't working.* The easiest products or services to sell are ones that compete against products or services that just don't work well enough. It's ideal if your product or service corrects a big problem. You might also have a product that improves a product drawback for one segment of the market or a product that offers significantly better benefits than current products.

9. *Market—definition and size.* Define the market and estimate its size. The market is where you do business. This can be defined by a geographic area, type of customers, and type of product. For a retail store, the market is a geographic area and a type of product. A paint store's market, for instance, would be the retail paint market in the western suburbs. For a manufacturer to businesses, the market is often the product category, price range, or performance characteristic of the product and a type of customer. For example, a company that sells satellite communication systems to truckers might have as its market high-end communication systems for over-the-road trucking firms. A service company would define its market by type of customer and service, such as a marketing consultant to emerging companies.

Make sure that your plan states that there's a dramatic opportunity for your product. People have to need or desire it. For example, When Ford introduced its Expedition sports utility vehicle (SUV), it made sure it was dramatically bigger than the Jeep Cherokee. The SUV that the Expedition replaced was the Explorer, which was the same size as the Cherokee. "Dramatic" means your product is at least 20% better than other products.

The size of the market should be defined in terms of the geographic area you serve and/or type of customers you serve. If you are currently serving a small segment of the market, for example, Chicago, but have long-term plans to serve a bigger market, you can list both the immediate market and the future market.

10. *Market—competition.* Who are the competitors and what are their strengths and weaknesses? Don't go into too much detail here about products that directly compete with yours; you should cover that in the Product section (Chapter 10). You want instead to focus on methods other than your type of product or service that people might use to meet their need or satisfy their desire. If there are a large number of reasons to compare, I prefer to have a chart that shows you have advantages over the competition.

11. *Market—distribution, number of channels, and how they work.* A distribution channel is the method that a product or service moves from your company to the point where the customer can buy it. In the case of a service company, distribution could be that you have a telemarketing sales force, a direct sales force, a marketing arrangement with another company, or an arrangement with independent sales representatives. A retail store's distribution includes its location, since that's the vehicle that brings products to the customer. But distribution could also include selling at shows, from a catalog, or through a direct sales force. For a manufacturer of hammers, for example, the channel might be general hardware distributors, specialty distributors selling to home improvement chains, or a network of manufacturers sales agents that sell to union carpenters.

> *If you ask investors, "What is the most important factor in marketing?" they will probably answer, "Distribution." Yet I consistently find plans that underestimate the difficulty of setting up distribution or, even worse, ignore distribution altogether. This is especially true if you're selling to retailers or businesses. It's also true for service businesses. Include your strategy for getting your product in front of customers so they can buy.*

*R*eaders will understand your plan much better when you reinforce your business strategy with an easy-to-understand rationale. Here the plan author emphasizes the reason the target is midsize companies: they have a need to effectively reach college students, but they don't have the resources to do that with large ad agencies. That comment sells the need for companies like PWS in the market and entices readers to believe in your plan.

Sample Section—Princeton WebSolutions

Business plan author: Michael Simmons, President and CEO.

Target Customers and Markets

Customer Profile

The primary customer profile is medium-sized businesses that have college students as part of their target market within 50 miles of New York City. The secondary customer profile will be advertising agencies and event promotion companies that work with medium- to large-sized businesses that have college students as part of their target market. The advertising agencies being targeted may or may not have an Internet consulting arm and our services will complement their services. While PWS will approach companies with national coverage, the primary focus of PWS will be companies with a strong regional focus. These companies typically can't afford large national budgets, but still have the money and need for reaching a regional audience.

The product categories of companies trying to reach college students include:

Travel Destinations	Cosmetics
Insurance	Banking
Fashion	Fashion Accessories
Entertainment	Job Recruitment
Malls/Department Stores	Dorm Room Products
Technology Products	Computer Sellers
Hair Salons and Barbers	Book Stores
Regional Restaurant Chains	Apartment Services

Alternative Education   Auto Dealers

Auto Repair   Extreme Sport Venues

Sporting Goods   College-Targeted Novelty

Music Stores   Products

Magazines/Newspapers

There is no practical estimate for the number of medium-sized businesses within 50 miles of New York, but PWS has been able to identify a minimum of 2,000 businesses that fall into its prospective customer criteria.

Customer Need

The need for unique approaches and programs for Generation Y, which includes college students, has been demonstrated by the large consumer-oriented companies and malls. Commenting on Generation Y, Cathy Grisham, Creative Director for KidCom, a division of Campbell Mithun Advertising, states, "All of the traditional marketing basics don't apply. They are more distrustful because they have grown up being marketed at." (*City Business*, June 30, 2000) Generation Y's computer expertise is another big difference. According to Cynthia Cohen, president of the market research firm Strategic Mindshare, "Gen Y's cognitive skills are highly developed. They have superb navigating skills on the (computer) and have no patience for poorly designed sites." (*Footwear News*, May 1, 2000)

Bigger companies have the resources to respond to the specific demands of Generation Y customers. Some examples include:

- The Glendale Galleria in Glendale, California has opened a $2.5-million wing called "The Zone," which features youth-oriented shops and a lounge with computers and TV sets.

Don't assume your readers will believe you are an expert on your market or your customers. List references, quotes from experts, and other source material to prove your point. The best information to include is quotes from interviews or other research you've conducted with end users. PWS's business plan would have been stronger with some feedback from customers, why they used PWS, and the results they received.

• The Block in Orange County, California is a $165-million shopping center that specifically targets Generation Y members.
• New retailers such as Skinmarket, which sells moderately priced cosmetics and accessories, have embraced the Generation Y market, with funky colors and stations where shoppers can try out the merchandise.
• Ralph Lauren introduced Ralph for Young Women, its first product targeted at Generation Y, with an entire new marketing approach, geared to the lifestyle and media savvy buying of Generation Y. To help the launch, freestanding turquoise blue iMAC computer terminals were installed in the store. Equipped with DVD players, the terminals broadcast computer easy graphics for Generation Y shoppers.

The problem for midsize companies is that they don't have the money or the expertise to reach out to Generation Y, which generates 10% of the consumer spending in the U.S. Probably one of the most important components of marketing to Generation Y is the Internet, where members go for a high percentage of all their market information.

While big companies can use the services of the giant advertising agencies like Campbell Mithun's KidCom, small and midsize companies are struggling to figure out just what to do.

College Student Internet Industry Overview

The current population of college students in 2000 is 12.8 million. This number is expected to go up to 13.4 million by 2003. The number of college students with

When you are selling to other businesses, it is a positive point to show why your customer group is in a strong growth market. After all, the better your customers do, the better you'll do. Here PWS talks about why the Internet is a growth opportunity for its target customer, mid-size companies marketing to college students over the Internet. Showing why the market is growing is also a strong indication that the customers will be willing to spend money on PWS's services.

Internet access is expected to go from 11.9 million (93%) to 12.7 million (95%) by 2003 (U.S. Census Bureau). The College Stores Research and Educational Foundation found that college students in the U.S. spend an average of $330 online each year. (QuickeStat, 2001) This means that in the year 2000, about $4,352,000,000 was spent by college students online. Also, it can be concluded that this number will increase as the college student population rises and advertisers become more effective at influencing students to buy online.

College students account for 43% of Generation Y that is online. (Forrester Research, 2000)

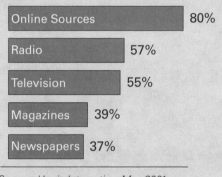

Online Sources 80%
Radio 57%
Television 55%
Magazines 39%
Newspapers 37%

Source: *Harris Interactive, May 2001*
© 2001 eMarketeer, Inc.

FIGURE 10-1. News media used by college students, 2001

As shown in Figure 10-1, 80% of new media usage by college students is done using online sources. This means that there is a large market in targeting college students who are Internet users.

Market Research and Conclusions

According to the market research, the Web development industry and the college student demographics

Front end and *back end* are common terms when dealing with the Internet. "Front end" refers to the user interface, when people access your site and then negotiate through it. "Back end" refers to the applications and databases that allow people to order and the company to process the order. Many companies are coordinating the back end of their Web systems with their current (also referred to as legacy) accounting and operations programs.

are both large and will be increasing for many years. The market is currently down and prices are lower than they were a year ago, but still higher than they were a few years ago. It is a great time to get into this space and establish footing with a robust business model as midsize companies are increasingly becoming aware of the need of reaching Generation Y.

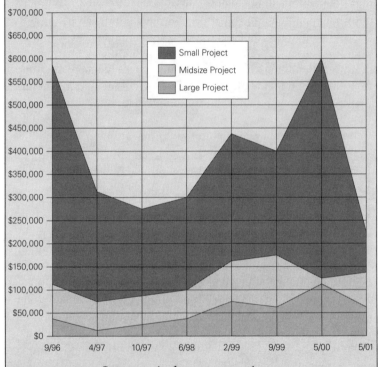

FIGURE 10-2. Internet industry overview

Market Analysis

Figure 10-3 shows where money that is allocated for Web development is being spent. The largest segment, of course, is "design and programming," which encompasses small, medium, and large Web sites. Many of the other aspects—such as network hardware, online trans-

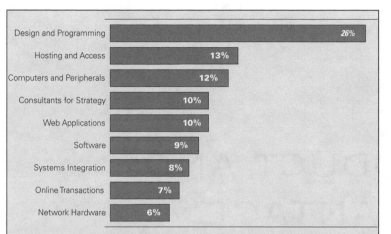

Source: *ActivMedia 2000* © 2001 eMarketeer, Inc.

FIGURE 10-3. Web site development budget allocation

actions, systems integration, and software—are being outsourced to Application Service Providers (ASPS). With this in mind, PWS is targeting the mid-size client companies that are interested in strategy consulting, design and programming, Web applications, and software. This market of B2B Internet services is projected to grow to $220 billion by 2003 (Forrester Research).

Competition

PWS's indirect competitors are the mid-size advertising agencies and Web developers that are used by mid-sized companies. There are many of these firms; over 40 are listed in the "Web Site Designer" section in the New York City Yahoo directory alone and there are 100s of freelance contractors that target medium-size companies. The potential for PWS's success is not that there are few competitors, but that PWS knows how to interact with college students, an understanding that the other agencies and Web developers lack. PWS will be selling its expertise creating Web pages for college students and its lower costs.

YOUR PRODUCT AND YOUR ADVANTAGE

WHAT MAKES YOU SPECIAL ◀

Your product is whatever you are selling: it doesn't matter if it's a service, a monthly maintenance, or a physical product people can touch and feel. If you have a retail store, your product is really the concept of the store and your merchandise, service, and layout are features of the store. For example, Home Depot's concept is a big home improvement store with plenty of expert assistance in "how-to" projects. Home Depot's prices, product selection, and location are all features of the stores.

In some cases, companies have a new technology that generates new products. If your technology is different, you should also have a section in the plan that discusses what your technology is, why it's better, and how you know it will work. New technology is a double-edged sword as far as investors are concerned. On the one hand, it offers the possibility of significant patent protection and a leading-edge position that could dominate the market. On the other hand, new technology rarely works as well as people anticipate, it often takes much longer to perfect than anyone expects, and it often has unexpected developments that kill the project.

Unless your company has tons of resources, I recommend you include your new technology as part of your product section. The emphasis of a plan needs to be on the customers and why the customers will want to buy your product.

In this section, you need to explain what your product is, how it relates to the customers' needs and desires, its pricing, its benefits, and how it compares to competition. You need to be careful not to give too much detail in this segment, as that will give the impression that your product is too complex and difficult to understand, which means that it will be hard to sell. Think instead of the one or two overriding reasons that a customer will buy your product and keep the focus of the section on those two points.

What to Communicate

1. *That your product is easy for customers to understand.* Prospective customers should be able to understand your product in less than 10 seconds, which means you should be able to describe it in fewer than 30 words. I believe this is an absolute requirement for a business plan, especially if you are raising money. If at all possible, try to show how your product's look or your company's logo and slogans help customers immediately understand what your product is and why it's better.

2. *That your product has an outstanding benefit that will make it easy to sell.* A key question any investor or banker asks about a business plan is "Will customers buy?" The best answer to the question is that you already have lots of customers buying. But in lieu of that, the best solution is to simply have a benefit that's clearly superior to anything competitors have.

3. *That, if your product sells through distribution, your prod-*

*E*ntrepreneurs often take space in their plans talking about how great a technology is or how strong a patent is. Investors and banks are worried about whether a product will sell. The strength of a technology is not as important as how you've positioned a product for sales. If you talk too much about technology, investors might believe that you feel your product "will sell itself"—something that rarely, if ever, happens.

> *Many business plans take the approach that there's simply no positive sales point that should be left unmentioned. All that does is make the plan too long, too wordy, and in the end very forgettable. People remember only two or three points, so make those points strongly. And then don't dilute your strong points by listing weaker benefits.*

uct meets the requirements of the distribution channel. Distribution channels are your first customer and you need to be sure you meet their requirements, which could mean going on peg board hooks or fitting onto a shelf of a specific size or being in the right price range for an upscale store. If you don't have actual job experience in your market, be sure to have an advisor who gives you the exact requirements of the channel.

4. *That your product concept is new or different in your target market.* You want to position your product as more than just another "me-too" entry into the market, but instead a new concept that better meets customers' needs and desires.

5. *That your product has significantly better benefits than competing products.* Your uniqueness isn't worth much if it doesn't translate into improved customer benefit(s). Hopefully, the benefit is 20% to 30% better than what the competition offers.

6. *That your product is strong enough to build a growing business in the future.* You want to convince investors and bankers that you're in business for the long haul. To do that, you need to show that your product line can be naturally expanded in the future to better meet the needs of your current customers or of new customer groups, so that your business can grow.

Format

1. *Describe your product line or set of services.* You may have several products or services, or in the case of a store, many departments. You need to list all of these services, but in a way that enforces that you are concentrating on one customer group or one market. The

ideal product line is one where each product adds to the others. For example, Claire's Boutique stores have several departments, including jewelry, cosmetics, and hair products, but they are all aimed at preteen and teen girls. The lines reinforce each other and add to the Claire Boutique credibility.

2. *Key Benefits.* List here the three main customer benefits of your product or service. These benefits should tie directly back to the customer needs or desires in your customers section.

3. *The overriding reason customers will buy.* In some cases, companies will have an exceptionally strong reason people will buy. Take the PT Cruiser, for example: the look—something different, something for the young—is the overwhelming reason for its success.

4. *Distribution channel requirements.* Distribution concerns don't exist with every product, but if your product will eventually end up on retailers' shelves, be sure to explain the criteria of the distribution channel(s) and how you meet them. You only want to cover the major requirements of distribution, which includes product packaging, discount terms, and marketing support.

5. *Show that you are better than your competition.* Don't go into too much depth on competitors, because you really want to sell your concept as unique. Dwelling on competition just seems to tell people that you aren't really that different. The only time I recommend you offer more than a paragraph or two on competition is when there are one or two dominant companies in the market. You need to be clear explaining why you have an opening to compete against those companies. You either need to have a

*W*rite your plan as if your readers know little about your industry. Don't use lots of acronyms without explaining what they mean and don't assume that readers will understand the functions of your features. Ask someone unfamiliar with your business to read the plan's product section and then see if he or she can explain what your product does. Cut back on industry jargon until any reader can understand your product.

feature or benefit that they don't have or you need a product that performs significantly better for one segment of the market.

6. *Your long-term future.* The best way to demonstrate is to show that your product or service is just the first step in satisfying the needs of your target customer group. The next best tactic is to show that you will be able to take your products and services out to new markets. Investors particularly want you to demonstrate that you have a long-term vision for the company that will grow sales five to 10 times over the next few years.

Sample Section—Princeton WebSolutions

Business plan author: Michael Simmons, President and CEO.

Products and Benefits

PWS offers Internet consulting and Web design and Web development programs.

Internet Consulting

PWS's main sales point is that it can help clients better reach college students because of its youth orientation. To reinforce that point, PWS's Internet consulting focuses first on helping clients understand how their customers perceive their Web sites. The main thrust of the PWS consulting program entails gathering information on a client's company, industry, market, customer, and client demographic and then planning how the client can most effectively use the Internet. PWS mixes market research and infiltration techniques to maximize the accuracy of the data collected. We also use accelerated creativity and brainstorming techniques in a total consulting process PWS calls Synergy Consulting, which is a cooperative event between PWS and the client to develop a creative Web site. PWS provides all or any one step individually to clients.

Phase 1: Discovery

This service gathers information on all aspects of how a company's Web presence is perceived and/or how a customer's Web presence should be delivered. PWS uses a wide variety of information collection methods, including *focus groups, field research, youth market infiltration,* and *online panels.* The goal of this phase is to produce a Field Assessment Report (FAR), which includes discussion of the optimum technology for the customer group, their needs, industry comparisons, market trends, creative potentials, and organizational assessments.

Phase 2: WebSolutions (Strategy)

The project manager uses the FAR research to develop an effective Internet strategy. WebSolutions is a series of idea stimulations and proven brainstorming methods, which rely on a combination of research and creativity. Every member of PWS is involved in the process to create the maximum results. The result of this phase is a clear-cut solution document called "Princeton's WebSolutions," which details how a client can use the Internet most effectively. The report also lists a price quote and timeline for each solution component.

Infiltration techniques and *infiltration marketing* refer to actually going out into the marketplace with customers and becoming one of them. For example, hosting concerts or contests and having guerilla teams of young people passing out samples and asking questions are infiltration tactics. This is in contrast to traditional techniques that simply observe what people do.

*W*hat's too much and what's too little? A great deal depends on your situation. In the case of PWS, the managers are in their early 20s and they need to convince readers that they have a sound approach. So this plan spends extra time explaining PWS's product concept so that readers can develop confidence. This would be too long for a management team whose experience itself creates investor confidence.

Phase 3: Defining the Scope of Work

Once the Web development contract and "Princeton's WebSolutions" have been approved by the client, the project manager provides the client with the proposed site architecture in the form of a basic HTML layout and a textual explanation. This architecture draft includes all of the pages that need to be developed for the site, their basic function, and how they link to one another. The project manager then works with the client to refine the site architecture to meet the client's exact specifications. Once the site architecture is determined, the client and project manager work together to define the content related to site, including end-user requirements, data modeling, media requirements, back-end programming, and all final objectives.

Phase 4: Initial Design

Using the project specification documents, the project manager passes the project on to the chief creative officer and the chief technology officer. In this phase, work is done on the Web site design and programming at the same time. The chief creative officer constructs optional layouts and works with the client to chose and finalize a visual direction. Concurrently, a beta version of the back-end of the Web page is created.

Phase 5: Implementation

Once the content, back-end system, and layouts are finalized, production begins. The PWS production team creates a prototype version of the site featuring full HTML versions with all the pages, multimedia, content, and back-end systems functioning.

In this phase, the client and PWS QA team sample

and review the prototype site. The client's feedback is received and implemented. The site is then debugged and approved for launch.

Phase 6: Evaluation Services

These services are in many ways similar to the discovery phase in that PWS can use a variety of market research activities to evaluate how end users perceived the site and how well the client's objectives are met by the site.

Web Design

Includes online branding, usability engineering, and multimedia. Online branding consists of the look, typography, content, logo, and any other messages the Web site sends to the end user. Usability engineering creates a Web site that is very easy to navigate and use. Web design is also an integral part of the initial design and implementation phases of Synergy Consulting, but the service is also offered separately for clients who have already created a Web page concept.

Web Programming

Includes the creation of e-business and custom Web applications, such as content management, customer relationship management, and e-commerce systems. These are services that also might be included in the complete Synergy Consulting program. They are separated so they can be offered separately to small and midsize companies that do most of the Web design and programming themselves but need help with the more complex back-end programming and implementation.

Both Web design and programming are services that are also meant to be lead-ins to the full Synergy

*M*any businesses have added products to take advantage of specific market opportunities that occur. As a result, their product lines appear to lack focus and direction. Writing a business plan is a good time to focus your products and your efforts on your main customer group. In the case of PWS, all three product lines are focused on the same target customer and they work together to promote PWS's main consulting business.

Consulting services. The target customer group frequently starts out by just looking for a Web programming service, either because they are unaware that consulting services exist or because they feel they can do their own Web page. Having these two services gives PWS the opportunity to talk to many more companies that are starting out on a Web development program.

Key Benefits

1. PWS knows college students and can help its clients maximize the impact created by their Internet-related marketing dollars.
2. PWS Synergy Consulting approach shares customer information with the client so that they can make a joint decision on how to proceed. This offers clients control of the Web development process and also provides clients insights they can use.
3. PWS is low cost, both in its consulting costs, as it is performed by students, and in its Web development costs, which is primarily outsourced overseas.

Competition

PWS's direct competition is Blabberforce (www.blabberforce.com), which is a student-run company that offers offline Gen Y marketing to companies, and Digimo (www.digimo.com), which is a student-run Web development company. In reality, these two companies help sell the concept that college students know what other college students want and have the technical know-how to produce the fast-paced Web sites college students want. There are more than enough customers for all three companies.

Make your benefit statements simple and clear-cut. Those are the points people can remember. PWS benefits are they know the customers, they are low cost, and they work cooperatively with clients. Those benefits are plenty strong and there isn't any need to go into greater depth than PWS has.

Future Products

PWS plans to expand its offerings to the college student market, first by expanding into markets other than New York and second by introducing new products and services, including:

- A portal Web site that keeps track of the latest buzz among college students and offers links to clients' sites;
- Tracking services about other sites that a site's visitors visit;
- Internet marketing strategies, including links to other sites, e-mail marketing, and target advertising;
- Conduct Internet contests, concerts, and other major events that clients can use to attract college students;
- Market research with college students on non-Internet projects, such as new products, surveys regarding buying decisions and buying habits, and research regarding market shares and marketing trends.

Investors and banks want your plan to provide a clear focus for the short term. After all, the long term isn't important if you don't succeed in the short term. But you still need to show you aspire to greatness. Be bold and don't worry about exactly how you'll achieve big future goals. All you need to do is have them and this is one of the sections where you can deliver the big picture of future growth.

MARKETING STRATEGY

Marketing's classic definition is the Four P's—price, promotion, product, and place, with place being another term for distribution. The product itself is covered in a separate section of the plan, which was covered in Chapter 10. The classic definition, though, leaves out positioning, which is a term describing how you present your product to customers so that they connect with the product. For example, products might be positioned as low cost, for the youth market, most dependable, rugged, adventuresome, or as the in thing to have. Price, promotion, product, and placement all work together to reinforce your positioning strategy, which is based upon what your target customer group wants or needs and on your product and how it's different from what your competition is offering.

Once you decide on a positioning strategy and figure out how to reinforce that strategy with the features of the product, including price, and the type of ads and promotion you'll run, marketing strategy deals with how to reach customers— through advertising, trade shows, the Internet, and other means—and determines how to actually sell the product.

The goal of this section is simply to explain your marketing strategy and the tactics you'll use to implement your strategy. The section is a little more detailed than others in the plan because of the importance most investors or banks will place on marketing.

What to Communicate

1. *That you understand that selling a product is never easy and that you have a comprehensive sales and marketing program.*

2. *That you are tapping into other resources through strategic alliances and/or distributors and sales agents to multiply the effectiveness of your marketing efforts.*

3. *That your marketing plan focus is on your customers' needs and desires first and your product second.* Your marketing strategy should show that it is geared to how customers buy, what they want to see, and how much support they need.

4. *That you have several tactics for locating and then selling to customers.* You need at least two to three approaches, especially if you are a new company, so that you have a better chance of finding a strategy that works effectively.

5. *That you have developed an effective positioning strategy to help customers understand the benefits of your product or service.*

6. *That you have an aggressive marketing program to bring in sales. Sales don't just happen.* If you expect sales results, you need an aggressive strategy.

7. *That your marketing tactics are cost-effective tactics that generate sales.* If your company is new, you want to avoid tactics that may not have immediate sales results, such as being a minor sponsor at a trade show

Most people assume they know all about marketing because they see advertising, they've attended trade shows, and people have sold them products. Those activities are only a part of marketing and they don't include positioning, which is the key to a successful campaign. Ignoring positioning in the plan will hurt your chances of attracting funding, as investors understand the crucial role it plays in a company's success.

or meeting. Concentrate on efforts that will produce sales.

Investors and banks will be very skeptical that the new company will be able to make sales at anywhere near its projected rates. The two ways to get around this skepticism are first to have someone with experience in the market on your management team and second to have an established network of contacts at key customers. List your network of contacts in the marketing section if you have any.

Format

1. *Explain your marketing objectives.* One of the purposes of a plan is for readers to see that you've thought out a plan and a strategy. They really can't tell how well you've designed your plan unless they know where you want to go. That's what your objectives tell them. Your objectives also give readers a chance to see that your strategy makes sense.

2. *Explain your positioning strategy, how you're projecting your product, service, or company to the customer.* Your strategy should clearly relate both to what your customers are looking for and to what your advantages are over the competition. This statement should be strong enough to make prospects notice you.

3. *List your positioning tactics.* Now that you have a strategy, be sure to list how you will communicate it to customers. This can be in your pricing, your packaging, your ad strategy, your targeted distribution strategy, and any number of other ways, such as slogans, logos, and product design. List only three or five of your major positioning tactics or the section gets to be too long.

4. *Tell how you will price your products.* You want to lay out the pricing for all of your major product lines, state how the prices have been determined, and what type of margin they will have. Pricing is a key product feature and should enhance the image of your company while at the same time providing significant profits for your company. I personally like to compare prices with those of competitors, either

direct or indirect. That gives readers a much better grasp of why your pricing is better.

5. *List the major methods you will use to promote your company.* You want to illustrate three points here. The first is that there are easy-to-implement tactics available to you, such as major trade shows or associations, well-read trade magazines, or Internet portal sites targeting your audience. The second is that you have low-cost tactics available. For example, a golf product manufacturer might list as a tactic "advertising in major golf magazines." The problem is those ads cost $25,000 to $50,000 each. So the plan should also mention low-cost regional retailer shows that cost only a few thousand dollars to attend. The last key point is that there's a wide variety of tactics you can implement. That conveys the message that if one program doesn't work, there are many others that might.

6. *Explain your distribution strategy.* This strategy explains how you're taking your product to end user customers so they can buy it. It could be through a direct sales force, through a strategic alliance, through either your own catalog or other catalogs, through the location of a store, or through distributors. In reality, there are hundreds of ways to distribute a product. In this section you want to show that you are using established, easy-to-penetrate distribution networks.

7. *Present your sales strategy and your reasons for choosing it.* This section should focus on how you plan on selling your product or service to the people who'll pay you for it. So if you sell to distributors, the sales strategy should focus on how you will sell to those distributors. If you sell through an alliance, the sales strategy should focus on how the alliance will sell to

Many new entrepreneurs put too much emphasis on advertising in their plans. Most advertising programs fail to cover their costs. I've seen some estimates that place the percentage of ads that fail between 80% and 90%. Your promotional program will make more sense to readers if it includes attendance at trade shows, seminars, contests, joint marketing efforts with other companies, or innovative uses of the Internet.

the customers who pay you, with a lesser emphasis on how you will set up an alliance. Try to include as much face-to-face contact as you can in your strategy. You'll find that many readers, especially investors, will take a dim view of telemarketing as a sales strategy unless it's already the norm in the industry.

Objectives need to be obtainable, specific, and at least somewhat measurable. PWS's objectives are straightforward and not all that dramatic, which is how they should be. If you set your objectives too high, readers might feel that you have a "pie in the sky" approach that is due to fail. While PWS's objectives may not be glamorous, readers will still realize PWS is stretching, as its goals aren't easy to achieve.

Section Sample—Princeton WebSolutions

Business plan author: Michael Simmons, President and CEO.

Marketing Strategy

Objectives

- Our initial marketing goal is to be running at least two concurrent profitable projects.
- Form meaningful, mutually beneficial partnerships with other interactive agencies, NYU, a public relations firm, a market research firm, and an online marketing firm.
- Update the PWS Web site (www.princetonwebsolutions.com) with new content and a newer look.
- Explore government contract possibilities for minority firms.
- Advertise at RFP (requests for proposals) exchanges and Web developer lists on the Internet.
- Create sales contacts with targeted midsize companies and land six clients in year one.

Positioning Statement

Princeton WebSolutions: Students helping clients reach students with cost-effective, guaranteed Web consulting and design.

Positioning Tactics

- Services are priced 35% to 50% lower than average market prices.
- Utilize students as sales people and account executives.
- Heavy emphasis on PWS's ability to test market concepts and generate feedback on Web sites with real college students.
- Company offers a guarantee. If the client is not satisfied by the quality of work we provide and the quality of service our project manager delivers, the client receives a 15% refund.

Pricing

In April 2000, the median hourly prices for Web development services in the New York City area were $150 for project management, $185 for strategy, $110 for production, $125 for copyrighting, $150 for design, $165 for multimedia, and $195 for U.S. programming and $85 for overseas programming. Taking into account the percentage decrease for the stock market, we can estimate that current prices are approximately 20% lower.

Based on this knowledge, we are pricing our services at less than 50% to 75% of the estimated industry rates. This would mean our rates are $60 for project management, $74 for strategy, $44 for production, $50 for copyrighting, $60 for design, $66 for multimedia, $78 for U.S. programming, and $40 for overseas pro-

Don't shortchange your information on pricing. Investors and banks are both concerned about margins, the money you make on each sale. One of the biggest mistakes I see in plans is that people believe they can charge more because they believe their product is better. Small companies are rarely able to charge more. You could end up without any margin at all if your prices are lower than what is listed in your plan.

gramming. Some of the services, which we offer at a fixed price, are based on these hourly rates.

All PWS prices are reduced 35% when sales are made through advertising agencies marketing to companies targeting Generation Y. These prices offer affordable savings to the agencies and support the marketing story of working with students (who don't draw the same top-dollar salaries as advertising agencies and experienced consultants) and offshore programming. This pricing strategy covers all operating expenses and salaries and invests over 20% of the money back into the company.

Consulting Services

Phase 1: Discovery	$5,000 to $10,000
Phase 2: WebSolutions	$2,500 to $10,000
Phase 3: Defining the Scope of Work	$2,500 flat fee
Phase 4: Initial Design	$5,000 to $15,000
Phase 5: Implementation	$40 or $78 per hour
Phase 6: Evaluation Services	$2,000 to $10,000

Web Design

$40 or $78 per hour

Web Programming

$40 or $78 per hour

Promotional Tactics

- PWS will advertise in the Web development section of Yahoo.
- PWS will register as a minority-owned business and pursue city, state, and federal contracts.
- PWS will advertise on Web development lists that advertise and organize Web developers.
- PWS will join and advertise on Web development RFP exchanges.

- PWS will join the Manhattan Chamber of Commerce, Toastmasters, Fat Thursday (Internet networking events), Association of Internet Professionals, SAEC (Silicon Alley Entrepreneurs Club), Alley Event (Internet-based events in the NYC area), Technet, BNI (Business Network International), The Breakfast Network, Silicon Alley Nights, and any other networking venues in New York City that have the potential of a good ROI.
- PWS will attend the "Teen Power Conference" in Florida 9/23-9/26 2001, the "Minority Council on Economic Development" in Maryland 9/21-9/26 2001, and the "Marketing to Youth Conference" in Canada in May 2002. PWS will attend other Internet- and Generation-Y-related conferences in the New York City area as they come up.
- PWS will start an online newsletter to send to existing clients and prospective clients to keep in touch with people and keep our brand awareness high.
- PWS will embark on a public relations campaign to get articles published in both business- and Internet-oriented New York City area magazines.
- PWS will create a college student Internet portal Web site. Based on our preliminary research, there is no Web site that aggregates all the information on this demographic as we plan to do. We plan to bring together articles, statistics, ratings on company Web sites that are currently trying to target college students, lists of events, and any other features that this market shows a need for.
- PWS will hold networking events specifically for advertising agencies and companies that target college students directly or indirectly. This event

A plan, especially by young people without a lot of experience, should show a willingness to work hard. PWS plan lists networking, which is inexpensive but time-consuming. Most importantly, networking is an effective way to meet new clients. As a rule, networking is more effective than direct mail, advertising, or telemarketing, especially when a company needs only five to 10 accounts.

If you need a plan to raise money, a good rule is to know what investors' perceptions are of various tactics. PWS's plan talks about having a portal site and networking events. Portal sites are considered expensive and difficult to implement. Networking events are considered effective and low cost. To gauge what's hot and what's not, read The Wall Street Journal *and magazines like* Inc., Entrepreneur, Fast Company, *and* Business 2.0.

will be for our niche and will be co-branded with other reputable firms so as to build our credibility.

Distribution Strategy

PWS has a two-prong distribution strategy. It will sell directly to companies that market to college students that are strong sales candidates for promoting their products through PWS's college student portal Web site. PWS will use sales over that site as an entry point for selling a wide variety of services. PWS can also offer those customers premium locations on the portal site.

PWS will sell its services through advertising and PR agencies for companies that currently aren't using the Internet as a primary marketing vehicle. These companies have established relationships with their clients and their clients will be easier to penetrate with a partner with established credibility.

Sales Strategy

- The entrance sales strategy will be focused on getting general clients through cold calls and networking contacts.
- Also being targeted will be government agencies, which must outsource 25% of their work to minority-owned businesses.
- Each employee will make two cold calls a day to prospective clients.
- PWS will start an alliance program where companies whose clients need Web development can co-brand our services and receive discounts on our services and the college student portal site that they can pocket or pass down to their customers.

Strategic Alliances

- PWS will form meaningful and mutually beneficial relationships with other interactive agencies and advertising agencies targeting Generation Y.
- PWS has talks under way to forming a partnership with ARC, a prestigious market research firm and one of our clients, and New York University.
- PWS will also form a partnership with one online marketing firm and one public relations firm so as to be able to offer clients a full range of services.

Sales Forecast

Years start in September.

2001 = $100,000

2002 = $400,000

2003 = $1,000,000

Every company has at least some characteristics that will be perceived as weaknesses. A plan should explain areas of perceived weakness in greater detail to demonstrate that the weakness won't hurt the company. PWS is a young company without a lot of sales and marketing experience. It offers more details on those activities to show readers that the perceived weakness won't affect the company.

13

COMPANY OPERATIONS AND MANAGEMENT

DOING THE RIGHT THINGS RIGHT ◀

Operations includes everything you do to buy, build, provide, or procure items or services in order to offer your product or service; it also includes administration functions you require to run your company. Operations sections of plans are dramatically different from plan to plan today, because businesses operate in so many different ways. Production is often outsourced to other companies and, in some cases, so are sales, marketing, administration, and human resource functions. For the most part, readers don't need all the information about how your operation works, but only information about the one, two, or three parts that will have a significant effect on your business. Typically two pages on operations is a long section.

The one part of business plans that hasn't changed for years is the management section. Good management will succeed in most businesses and bad management can turn even the best business concepts into business failures. Of course, management has to start somewhere and there have been many successful businesses started by young or inexperienced entrepreneurs. If at all possible, you want to be able to show your management has a successful background. If you don't have that experience, you need to show that management has dedication and enthusiasm and that you have found mentors who will help you.

This section shows you have thought through the different aspects of your business and that your management team is strong. As a rule, your Operations section gets a rather cursory read but your Management section gets close scrutiny. There are two times when Operations becomes a key issue: first, when people may worry that you cannot get the key employees you need for manufacturing or technology positions, and second, when your overhead expense is so high that it threatens the survival of the company.

What to Communicate

1. *That you have minimized the company's risks.* You do this by outsourcing or having low upfront costs for production and administrative functions. You want the money going into your company to be used as much as possible for marketing, sales, and management.

2. *That your managers have experience or access to the management advisors they need to keep the company running smoothly.*

3. *That you have an effective personnel compensation plan to keep top employees and management.* This is especially true if you are recruiting employees who are difficult to find.

4. *That you have thought through the key operations issues that will affect your business.* If possible, you want to show a relationship between the resources you devote to operations and the potential sales you will have. For a new company, try to keep both management costs and overhead expenses to about 25% of your total expenses.

5. *That you have made a strong effort to keep your fixed costs as low as possible.* New companies especially should show they are subletting office space from an existing

> *Don't assume that readers (especially investors and bankers) will believe that your success in one business is a predictor of success in another business. Each market has unique challenges and people are most interested in seeing that you have experience in the market of your current business. If you don't have that experience, do everything you can to get an employee or mentor with the proper experience.*

The greatest skill managers have is their ability to respond to problems. If you are short of experience, show that your management team has adjusted to problems in the past. One of the problems with the emphasis on management experience is that it implies that managers can know everything. That's not true. What they do know is how to recognize a problem and how to create a response to that problem.

company or taken other steps to keep overhead costs down. It's a red flag to investors when you want to lease expensive office or manufacturing space when you don't have enough revenue.

Format

Operations sections don't have a standard format and can discuss any relevant part of the company's operations. For your operations section, chose the points listed here as appropriate for your business. The last three points—10, 11, and 12—refer to management. These can be broken out into a separate section, as in the Sample Section on Princeton WebSolutions, or they can be included in the Operations section.

1. *Identify the company's place of business.* Give the address and a brief description of the business.

2. *Give a short description of how goods or services are produced or procured.* Explain any outsourced operations. If goods are made by you, indicate whether your services are provided by employees or independent contractors. Give any other information that is unusual about how you produce your goods or services.

3. *If materials or services are purchased, explain the source of supply and any favorable pricing terms that you've negotiated.* This is particularly important for retail stores, for which the plan needs to detail pricing from vendors and how it compares with pricing for other area retailers. Restaurants also offer more details on procuring specialty food if that's an important part of their business.

4. *Offer a short description of any outsourced arrangements you have.* This should explain any contracts or agreements you have, pricing arrangements, and payment

terms. Be sure to list clearly any favorable arrangements you have from vendors, including extended credit, a large line of credit, or amortized tooling or other cost-sharing arrangements.

5. *Explain how you've aligned your operations to keep overhead low.* This is especially important if you have a high overhead business, like a manufacturing operation or a retail store.

6. *If you need to purchase capital equipment or you expect major computer expenses, you should detail what those expenses are, why they are needed, and how they will help increase your bottom line.*

7. *For retail stores, talk about their location—why it's advantageous, what it costs, and how it supports the company's marketing campaign.*

8. *Explain your personnel hiring and training policies.* A company's success depends greatly on the quality of the people it hires. You should explain not only how you will get the best employees, but how you will retain, train, and motivate them. This section should also include information about any stock incentives or bonus programs.

9. *Give a brief description of administrative functions, with costs.* An existing company should show administrative functions of 10% or less of sales revenue.

10. *List key members of your management team and provide a paragraph of information about each.* You can choose to list in the appendix complete résumés of your managers, though it is not necessary.

11. *List members of your board of directors, with a brief biography about each one's experience.*

12. *List the members of your board of advisors, if you have one.*

> **Amortized costs** refers to a situation in which a vendor or someone else pays upfront costs for equipment or tooling and then receives its money back on a per-unit or monthly basis to pay back the vendor. For example, a vendor might pay $25,000 for tooling and then charge the customer an extra 10 cents per unit until the tool is paid for. Check with any outsourced vendor to see if they will offer you amortized costs in order to receive your business.

An experienced financial executive is one of the key employees investors and banks look for, because it helps them believe money issues will be handled responsibly. Unfortunately, it's also a position that many entrepreneurs tend to minimize or overlook because the position doesn't produce any revenue. If you need to raise money, be sure to at least have a board member or advisor with financial experience.

Section Sample—Princeton WebSolutions

Business plan author: Michael Simmons, President and CEO.

Operations

Operational Philosophy

PWS's operational approach is based on a three-prong mission. The first is to offer students unique learning opportunities in an entrepreneur environment. Students working for PWS not only get to work within the PWS operating environment, but they get to work closely with clients as they work at clients' and prospects' offices in order to better understand their business. The second prong is to help client companies better understand the college student market by offering a wide variety of market research tools and by loaning students to companies to work with them on their marketing programs. The third prong is to provide cost-effective Web development programs by offering in-depth support with an all-out effort to constantly communicate with its clients. The result is that clients feel in control of the development process.

PWS has gone to this three-prong approach because it is good for the student, good for the clients, and good for PWS. The student gains because he or she participates in a great learning environment. The clients gain because they have on-site access to their student customers' viewpoints and input regarding the latest techniques being taught in the country's leading business schools, and because they will save money. The company gains because students will be highly motivated to learn and because they will work for less money than they could get elsewhere.

Overseas Programming

PWS students' main focus is consulting, project management, and the entrepreneur environment. PWS does not plan on having students or staff do the actual programming work. It will be outsourced to local programming firms, freelance Web page designers, and overseas programming firms. Over the past two years, PWS has developed eight relationships with different development firms located in India, Finland, and Pakistan with plans of significantly increasing such relationships. PWS has also developed a communication infrastructure that allows it to interface effectively with these teams and finish high-quality projects on budget. Strategically outsourcing also allows PWS the ability to downsize when the market shrinks as well as to easily take on more client work in up markets.

Personnel Development

PWS will hire the top students from the top universities in the New York City area. Positions include sales representatives, project managers, and unpaid interns. High-achievers will be targeted and recruited in the first semester of their freshman year to begin work in the second semester. Freshmen or other people starting out with PWS will first go through an unpaid internship in which they are trained in self-development and PWS's company's goals and business operations. Part of these internships will include getting involved in several real projects, including spending time at prospective or current clients' operations.

> *E*verybody wins. Business models where everyone wins are typically pretty appealing to just about everyone. The PWS model has tried to create a winning situation for all parties by not just using students as employees, but also offering both students and clients a learning experience. This extra twist adds another dimension to the typical Web development business, a dimension that's both interesting and potentially very profitable.

*D*on't be afraid to deviate from a standard business plan format in order to emphasize a unique angle of your business. PWS goes into greater depth about how it will motivate and train its employees because that's a twist. The special emphasis ensures that readers will note this twist; plus, it shows the company has a commitment to implementing this strategy.

After graduating from the internship level, student employees will receive mentoring and field training from other employees, results-based income, and self-development seminars. On top of this, students will have the opportunity to shadow clients and potential clients as they work and learn more about business from a different perspective, while learning about the clients' needs at the same time. As employees go through their college experience, they will have the opportunity to move up within the company, get compensated based on results, go on business trips across the nation, and become mentors and field trainers to younger employees. One of the goals for PWS in terms of hiring people is that working for PWS becomes a highly sought-after job. The PWS plan is to create something comparable in terms of students willing to work for less in order to have a life-changing experience.

When these employees graduate from college, they will have three choices. They can choose to work full-time at PWS, start their own branch of PWS, or get another job. PWS partnerships will include businesses within the community and clients, so that the best possibilities for jobs will be open to student employees no matter which direction they decide to take.

According to Vector Marketing, the average college student makes $2,000 a year. A major PWS assumption is that college students will be willing to have low salaries in return for experience, credentials, and training.

As part of the business, there will be a closely linked PWS school club. For this club, we will recruit speakers, ask advisory and board members to speak, and have management give self-development seminars to employees. The NYU-funded club, which is currently operating, is a great introductory way for people to learn about the job. During the summer and winter breaks, clubs will offer self-development conferences that employees can attend that will be held at resorts and other vacation destinations. Top-performing students will be sponsored to attend Operation Enterprise (www.amanet.org/oe), NFTE (www.nfte.com) summer programs run by the American Management Associa-tion, and other leadership and self-development seminars.

Administrative Functions

Currently, administrative functions are handled by management. As the company grows, these functions will be either outsourced or set up as intern learning opportunities within NYU and other New York City area universities.

Management

Management Team

Michael Simmons. Currently attending his sophomore year at the Stern School of Business at NYU, Michael is a co-founder and partner of Princeton WebSolutions. He is experienced in self-development, Web development, and knowledge management and has worked for such companies as Operation Enterprise, the young adult division of the American Management Association.

For the year 2000, Michael was awarded the prestigious "Young Entrepreneur of the Year Award" for New York City and the East Coast Collegiate Entrepreneur Award for New York. He was also

> *I recommend that every company looking for large amounts of money have a board of directors, or at least a board of advisors, even if, as in the case of PWS, one person owns the company. The board offers insight and alternative views for major decisions and forces the owner to defend his or her decisions. This added input helps protect the owner from making mistakes.*

> *A major mistake that many entrepreneurs make is to have too many members of management who have similar backgrounds and personalities. People are always most comfortable with people who are like themselves. What you want, though, in a management team, is balance with a variety of personalities and viewpoints, so that each decision is made only after understanding all ramifications of the decision.*

recently named to the board of the Entrepreneur Exchange Group at the Stern Business School. Michael can be contacted directly at michael@princeton-netsolutions.com.

Daniel Blank. Currently attending his sophomore year at the Stern School of Business at NYU and majoring in marketing, Daniel recently joined PWS as the Chief Creative Officer. He has taken Web development classes at NYU and has had several internships in the new media industry, where he helped create several Web sites.

Rishi Chhabria. Rishi currently is a junior at the Stern School of Business at New York University. He is the Chief Business Development Officer of PWS and will be integral in raising funds and forming partnerships. Rishi is a Finance and Marketing major, and is experienced in accounting, networking strategies, and graphic design. He has worked for such investment companies as The Heartland Advisors and A.G. Edwards and has held a part-time job doing graphic design for New York University Athletics. Rishi has ascertained his knowledge by constantly expanding his knowledge through constant social interaction, and reading investment books and magazines.

Rishi has spent much of his life as a leader. Over the past several years, he has been treasurer of his high school, vice president of the National Honor Society, and president of the Varsity Club. Rishi has also held two cabinet positions in his fraternity, Phi Gamma Delta.

Richard Salem. Chief Marketing Officer. Originally from Honolulu, Hawaii, Richard Salem attends New

York University, where he is currently pursuing a degree in Journalism and Mass Communications with a minor in Computer Science. For the past year, Salem has worked as an Innovation Specialist for PWS. As an Innovation Specialist, his duties included consulting, public relations, content editing, marketing, Web development, market research, and client relations. Some of his key achievements for the year 2000 include helping on PWS's new Generation Y targeted marketing strategy, development of the new company Web site, and event coordination for the Fleet Youth Entrepreneur Expo at which PWS received first place.

Salem spent the summer gaining valuable marketing and sales experience as a Senior Advisor for Vector Marketing, an international marketing firm. Honored as the Top Sales Representative (#1 out of 150+), Salem trained numerous sales representatives and teams in high-performance sales, customer relations, phone time, and the art of modeling.

Board of Advisors

PWS does not yet have a board of advisors, but it plans on forming one in the very near future. Advisors will be chosen by their industry, expertise, and network of contacts.

FINANCIAL SECTION

WHERE THE MONEY COMES FROM AND WHERE IT GOES ◀

The financial section of the plan is the key area, where people will judge just how competent you are as a business manager. The financial portion of any business plan should be well written, sufficiently documented, and concise and it should follow these rules:

- Financial projections must tie into and be consistent with the narrative sections of the business plan—and will in a large part depend upon the stage and goals of the company.

- Financial projections must tie in with historical numbers and, to the extent that they do not, discrepancies should be explained. For example, if sales have been flat during the last three years, but are projected to grow at 35% per annum, you must explain how and why.

- Financials should be prepared with a specific reader or audience in mind. For example, lenders are interested in cash flow and sources of repayment, investors will focus more closely on EBITDA, and strategic partners may look at the balance sheet. (Note: this chapter assumes that the reader of the business plan is an investor or a lender.)

Much of the information in this was chapter was furnished by: Jim Lewin, BizPlanIt, 7702 E Doubletree Ranch Road, Suite 300, Scottsdale, AZ 85258, 480-970-6161,www.bizplanit.com.

- Use charts and graphs to summarize key financial information, highlight important figures, and keep the reader interested.
- All financial statements should be prepared on an *accrual* basis, rather than on a *cash* basis—it's how businesses are managed and provides the best picture for sophisticated readers. With an accrual basis, you report sales when the sale is made or an item is purchased, and not when you actually receive or pay the money. With a cash basis, businesses simply report when cash actually comes in or goes out.

The purpose of this section is to explain to readers your future sales and profitability. Of special interest will be your margins, your breakeven point, how fast profits ramp up as sales increase, and your downside potential if sales drop off. The section also explains how you will spend money, if you are requesting it, and if applicable, what type of offer you are making to investors.

> **EBITDA** stands for "earnings before interest, taxes, depreciation, and amortization." Depreciation is the amount by which you discount equipment every year it is used. Amortization is similar to depreciation in that you write off a major expense based on use. For example, you might amortize tooling based on production if the tool will produce only 150,000 units. A high EBITDA occurs when you have high margins and low expenses.

What to Communicate

1. *That you understand financials and the financial process.* This understanding is essential if you're trying to raise money.
2. *That your business will produce significant profits and that your margins are high.*
3. *That your business shows steady profit growth as sales increase.*
4. *That you will manage your finances wisely, using both your current resources and any future investments or loans.*

Format

The financial portion of a business plan can often be organized into four parts:

1. *A financial review of the current/historical status of the company*
2. *Financial assumptions that form the basis for the projected numbers*
3. *Three to five years of projected financial statements*
4. *An optional Financial Summary section*

Financial Review

Begin with a description of the company's current financial status in which you explain the current and historical condition of the business. It is important to focus on strengths and weaknesses inherent in the numbers—particularly for areas where performance is significantly better or worse than might be expected. Explain, for instance, that a change in pricing strategy proved to be an error that resulted in a loss for the quarter, but after realizing the mistake, management reverted to its prior pricing formula. After highlighting those points that warrant discussion, provide a table to summarize key balance sheet and income statement accounts for the past three years (Figure 14-1).

*M*any entrepreneurs will have their financials prepared by a consultant or an accountant. Often the result is that they don't understand the assumptions behind the financials. It's crucial for owners to understand the assumptions, projections, and ramifications of those numbers when preparing the plan. Employing a consultant to prepare a business plan and financial projections is often helpful, but owners still need to understand their numbers.

	1998	1999	2000
Total Assets	$4,390	$4,788	$5,562
Stockholders' Equity	$1,998	$2,567	$3,445
Revenues	$18,920	$20,244	$22,066
Gross Profit	$9,007	$10,875	$11,342
EBITDA	$2,270	$2,456	$2,648

FIGURE 14-1. XYZ Company financial summary (figures in thousands)

Financial Assumptions

Begin this section by carefully reviewing all of the under-lying assumptions that form the basis of the financial pro-jections. Like the projections, financial assumptions must be reasonable, thoughtful, and defendable. Assumptions are the numbers you use for calculating your financial statements. For example, you might assume sales will grow 10% per year, the cost of goods will stay at 44%, and sales, marketing, and administrative expenses are 22% of sales. State and then defend your assumptions in each section.

A. Income Statement Assumptions

Sales. Sales assumptions determine the overall level of growth for the business. Many other important assump-tions will be tied into sales assumptions, such as balance sheet and cash flow assumptions. When developing sales projections for more than one product or product group, it's often useful to organize those products or groups into sep-arate categories or line items. Similarly, if the company sells one product but in distinctly different markets, the sales should be categorized by market. This is particularly impor-tant information for a reader of your plan. Figure 14-2 shows two examples:

oxes, graphs, or simple charts are by far the most convincing display of financial information. It is also how most other plans display financial information. Try to incorporate at least three to four boxes into your financial section. Be sure your ratios, especially gross profits and EBITDA, are in line with the ratios of other compa-nies in the industry. Large libraries will have reference books on standard industry ratios; the best ones are from Prentice Hall.

Revenues		Revenues	
Systems	$20,500	United States	$12,500
Software	$3,000	International	$11,000
Total Revenues	$23,500	Total Revenues	$23,500

FIGURE 14-2. Sales

Cost of Sales. Readers want to compare production costs, which would be inventory cost for a retailer and cost of service personnel for a service company, of the company to another similar company to determine if your business has

*C*ost of goods sold should receive special emphasis in every plan, as it is an important financial figure. You can cut marketing, overhead, and administrative expenses, but it's hard to change how much it costs to produce or procure what you sell. Cost of goods sold also determines the gross margin, which is the percentage of sales left after deducting the cost of goods sold.

Income statements state sales less all expenses to determine income. *Balance sheets* show a company's assets and liabilities, both short term and long term, along with shareholders' equity. *Cash flow statements* show how much cash a company has on hand at any time. See Appendix A for an example of an income statement, a balance sheet, and a cash flow statement. These are the three key statements every business plan needs.

efficient manufacturing or production costs.

If a company has been in business for a number of years and knows its cost of sales run at 39% of sales, then future assumptions should reflect that ratio. If on the other hand, the enterprise being planned is a start-up, or is moving into a new facility, the cost of sales must be carefully broken down into each of its components. For example, cost of sales categories might include material cost, direct labor, utilities, transportation and overhead expenses of a manufacturing facility.

- **Research and Development.** If there is an R&D element to the business, you need to discuss how much capital is allocated to R&D, usually expressed as a percentage of sales. R&D represents a company's investment in its future, so readers—particularly investors—may be quite interested in this figure.

- **Marketing Expense.** In many younger companies, marketing expenses play a large role and early-stage investors will assume that a large portion of the capital being raised will go towards marketing to establish a brand or sell products. Heavier marketing costs are often expected for younger companies, so detail these expenses for each year of the planning period. If marketing costs are not a major expense item, they can be included with items in the next category, General and Administrative expenses.

- **General and Administrative Expenses (G&A).** Total G&A is an important figure because subtracting it from gross profit will determine the company's profitability. G&A consists of a number of accounts that are usually small in relation to the total, and often fixed. In the assumptions paragraph on G&A you should discuss any unusually large accounts, for example salaries, rent or entertainment expenses.

You also need to detail any significant G&A changes from historical financial performance.

- **Taxes.** If the plan is for a relatively mature company, then an independent accountant should be requested to prepare the tax assumptions, including topics such as type of corporation and method of accounting. If, on the other hand, a company is new or emerging, a discussion of tax issues may not be relevant.

B. Balance Sheet Assumptions

- **Inventory.** The assumption should include how many inventory turns are expected each year. Additionally, there should be a discussion about the relationship of inventory to cash and how practices like "just-in-time" will be utilized. This is applicable primarily for retail and manufacturing firms.

- **Accounts Receivable.** If you have commercial customers, it is likely there will be significant A/R. In this case, the assumption should advise if A/R is projected with a time period, which refers to the days you need to collect receivables, such as 60 days. Many companies that require 60 days or longer to collect payment borrow against their A/R to increase working capital. Explain any plans you have to do this in this section.

- **Investments.** If a company intends to raise a round of financing, this assumption will detail how funds will be invested until they are needed in the business.

- **Property and Depreciation.** This assumption should discuss large assets the company has acquired, or expects to acquire during the planning period. It is helpful to describe how assets will be financed, if financing strategies are known. Also, advise the reader about how assets will be depreciated.

> *If you are a start-up, be careful too avoid adding fixed G&A expenses. For example, instead of hiring an accountant with a fixed salary, hire an outside accountant whose fees vary depending on the work level. Sales often take longer to develop than entrepreneurs expect and G&A expenses can cost a company all of its development money before sales develop.*

*D*on't become confused by the word assumptions when talking about financials. In many cases, the assumptions are facts. That you have a bank loan and what the terms consist of are certainly facts. I've heard new entrepreneurs answer the question, "What financial assumptions have you made?" with "We haven't made any." Some parts of your financial section are facts and other parts are assumptions, but they're all called assumptions.

- **Debt.** If the company has credit facilities with banks, finance companies or leasing companies, it should be disclosed here. Information on terms, amortizations, maturity dates, collateral, and interest costs should be disclosed in this assumption.

Financial Projections

Most business plan readers expect to see three to five years of financial projections. Less than three years is considered too short a planning period to understand a company's goals and longer than five years is often not considered to be meaningful. Financial projections should include an income statement, a balance sheet, and a cash flow statement. It's typically best to present financial projections on an annual basis, along with the prior two or three years if available, to allow readers to easily compare projections with historical performance. Many readers, particularly lenders, will also be interested in reviewing the first year or two on a monthly basis, included on separate sheets.

Many investors and banks believe that EBITDA is the best way to compare one company with another—even companies in different industries. EBITDA tells a reader how much money a company makes or loses from its operations. Therefore, it's the fairest way to evaluate a company's prospects, and I recommend that you present an EBITDA summary in a graph format in your plan (Figure 14-3).

Financial Summary

This section summarizes the overall financial results of the plan and is often included instead of or also in the Executive Summary. This section may also be used to introduce other financial information that may be useful, including the following:

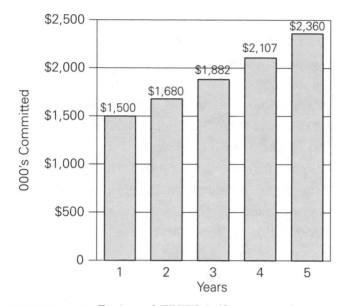

FIGURE 14-3. Projected EBITDA (figures in thousands)

- **Financial Ratios.** A business plan, especially for an established company might provide certain financial ratios for the most current year-end statements, or perhaps for all of the years during the planning period. Depending upon the type of business, certain ratios are more important than others. Some of the more widely used ratios include:
  - *Quick Ratio:* By dividing the sum of cash and accounts receivable by current liabilities, a reader can ascertain the company's liquidity. The larger the ratio, the more liquid the company is considered to be.
  - *Current Ratio:* This ratio enables the reader to understand a company's ability to pay its bills. Divide current assets by current liabilities to calculate.
  - *Total Assets to Net Worth:* This leverage ratio varies greatly from industry to industry. However,

*A*n established ongoing business will typically include the ratios described here because they know them from experience. For a new business these ratios are all speculation. Don't show these ratios if you can't be sure what they will be. Instead concentrate on your EBITDA and your expected sales growth. The story you want to tell is you have a huge marketing opportunity and your gross margins will be high.

when dividing total assets by net worth, a smaller number is always preferred—indicating the company is not too highly leveraged. The best way to judge this ratio is in comparison to other companies within a similar industry.

– *Collection Period:* Accounts receivable divided by sales and then multiplied by 365. If the result is higher than the selling terms (say 30 days), then the company may not be effectively collecting receivables.

– *Net Sales to Inventory:* By dividing sales by inventory, the reader can analyze how efficiently a company is using its assets. Generally, the higher the number the better.

– *Assets to Sales:* This ratio tells the reader if a company is gaining the most benefit from the capital that management is investing in the business.

– *Accounts Payable to Sales:* By dividing A/P by annual sales, a lender or supplier can determine if a company is using its suppliers to help finance operations. The lower the number, the better.

– *Return on Sales:* Also known as *profit margin*. By dividing net profit by annual sales, the reader learns the amount of profit generated from each dollar of sales.

– *Return on Assets:* Like most ratios, this one varies by industry. However, this ratio can tell the reader how efficiently a company is using assets and if it deserves additional capital to expand further.

– *Return on Equity:* If the reader divides net profit by net worth, he or she can conclude if additional capital will receive an acceptable return.

Funding Request

This is a statement of the amount of money being raised and the terms of the offer; for example, a convertible note, a loan, or sale of stock.

Use of Proceeds

This section provides an opportunity to give readers further detail related to the amount and uses of capital that is either being borrowed or raised.

Exit Strategy

Investors want to know how they can get money out of an investment. Typical scenarios are an initial public offering, a merger with a larger company, or, in the case of a convertible bond or loan, terms for when the bond or loan will be repaid.

Funding Request, Use of Proceeds, and Exit Strategy are typically included only in plans when entrepreneurs are seeking money from investors.

Sample Financial Statements

Figures 14-4, 14-5, and 14-6 show a sample income statement, a sample balance sheet, and a sample cash flow statement prepared by and reproduced with the permission of BizPlanIt, www.bizplanit.com.

Every business plan should be written with a specific audience in mind. While plans are often written to raise money, other appropriate audiences could include a company's senior management team, company employees, suppliers, strategic partners or key customers. The financial overview section of a business plan must be tailored to answer the specific questions and needs of your audience. It should be especially thorough if you are looking to borrow money from a bank.

	Year 1	Year 2	Year 3	Year 4	Year 5
Revenue					
Product #1 Revenue	168,750	1,837,500	6,670,000	16,447,500	33,525,000
Product #2 Revenue	16,875	498,750	2,355,000	7,925,000	20,887,500
Service Revenue	3,000,000	6,240,000	12,480,000	24,300,000	44,400,000
Total Revenues	3,185,625	8,576,250	21,505,000	48,672,500	98,812,500
Total Cost of Sales	46,606	584,063	2,256,250	6,093,125	13,603,125
Gross Profit	3,139,219	7,992,187	19,248,750	42,579,375	85,209,375
Operating Expenses					
Employee Expenses					
Operational Payroll	2,731,511	5,089,437	7,836,488	13,709,345	19,142,322
Payroll Taxes and Benefits	819,453	1,526,831	2,350,946	4,112,804	5,742,697
Recruiting Expenses	10,000	20,000	20,000	30,000	30,000
Total Employee Expenses	3,560,964	6,636,268	10,207,434	17,852,149	24,915,019
Marketing/Sales Expenses					
Marketing Expenses	380,414	1,090,688	2,309,156	3,838,875	5,961,094
Channel Partner Fees	67,500	735,000	2,668,000	6,579,000	13,410,000
Travel/Entertainment	120,000	240,000	240,000	360,000	360,000
Total Marketing Expenses	567,914	2,065,688	5,217,156	10,777,875	19,731,094
Total Web Site and Technology	321,750	324,800	418,050	555,300	756,300
Total General and Administrative	409,740	963,156	1,926,025	3,783,724	6,935,062
Total Operating Expenses	4,860,368	9,989,912	17,768,665	32,969,048	52,337,475
Net Operating Income (EBITDA)	(1,721,149)	(1,997,725)	1,480,085	9,610,327	32,871,900

FIGURE 14-4. Income statement (continued on next page)

	Year 1	Year 2	Year 3	Year 4	Year 5
Financial Expenses					
Depreciation	46,333	117,500	213,000	393,667	599,000
Pre-Tax Net Profit (Loss)	(1,767,483)	(2,115,225)	1,267,085	9,216,660	32,272,900
Income Taxes	0	0	0	2,508,394	12,263,702
Net Income (Loss)	(1,767,483)	(2,115,225)	1,267,085	6,708,266	20,009,198
Cumulative Net Profit (Loss)	(1,767,483)	(3,882,708)	(2,615,623)	4,092,643)	24,101,841

FIGURE 14-4. Income statement (continued)

	Year 1	Year 2	Year 3	Year 4	Year 5
ASSETS					
Current Assets					
Cash	2,757,104	(66,834)	1,904,473	6,018,164	21,295,997
Accounts Receivable	381,747	847,959	1,866,738	4,054,979	8,215,344
Total Current Assets	3,138,851	781,126	3,771,211	10,073,143	29,511,341
Property/Equipment	193,667	436,167	713,167	1,119,500	1,690,500
Total Assets	3,332,517	1,217,292	4,484,377	11,192,643	31,201,841
LIABILITIES AND STOCKHOLDERS' EQUITY					
Liabilities					
Current Liabilities					
Accounts Payable	0	0	0	0	0
Total Current Liabilities	0	0	0	0	0
Total Liabilities	0	0	0	0	0
Stockholders' Equity					
Paid-in Capital	5,100,000	5,100,000	7,100,000	7,100,00	7,100,000
Retained Earnings	(1,767,483)	(3,882,708)	2,615,623)	4,092,643	24,101,841
Total Stockholders' Equity	3,332,517	1,217,292	4,484,377	11,192,643	31,201,841
Total Liabilities and Stockholders' Equity	3,332,517	1,217,292	4,484,377	11,192,643	31,201,841

Note: This model assumes that all accounts payable are paid in the month in which the expense is incurred.

FIGURE 14-5. Balance sheet

	Year 1	Year 2	Year 3	Year 4	Year 5
Revenues	3,185,625	8,576,250	21,505,000	48,672,500	98,812,500
Cash Inflows					
Collection of A/R	2,803,878	8,110,038	20,486,222	46,484,258	94,652,135
Proceeds from Sale of Stock	5,100,000	0	2,000,000	0	0
Total Cash Inflows	7,903,878	8,110,038	22,486,222	46,484,258	94,652,135
Cash Outflows					
Payments on A/P	4,906,774	10,573,975	20,024,915	39,062,174	65,940,600
Payments for deposits	0	0	0	0	0
Payments to Purchase Equipment	240,000	360,000	490,000	800,000	1,170,000
Income Tax Payments	0	0	0	2,508,394	12,263,702
Total Cash Outflows	5,146,774	10,933,975	20,514,915	42,370,568	79,374,302
Net Cash Flows	2,757,104	(2,823,938)	1,971,307	4,113,691	15,277,833
Cash, Beginning of Period	0	2,757,104	(66,834)	1,904,473	6,018,164
Cash, End of Period	2,757,104	(66,834)	1,904,473	6,018,164	21,295,997

FIGURE 14-6. Cash flow statement

Section Sample—Princeton WebSolutions

Business plan author: Michael Simmons, President and CEO.

Financial

Financial Review

The company has had two years where it has test-marketed its concept while finalizing its strategic alliances and marketing and operational practices. During that time, the company has been able to establish it can keep its margins and expenses in line to produce an EBIT (earnings before interest and taxes) in the 15% range. The company is debt-free and will be funded by the principals and the sale of stock.

Financial Assumptions

- **Sales.** The sales period is from September 1 to August 31 of the following year.

2001-2002	$100,000
2002-2003	$400,000
2003-2004	$1,000,000

  Sales are projected to increase from $100,000 through the recruitment of sales personnel, the improvement of the portal Web site, and the success of the jobs the company lands.

- **Cost of Goods Sold.** PWS is pricing its services for a 50% margin. PWS has arranged with its outsourced vendors for pricing that produces this margin while still offering customers a price 25% to 50% lower than its competitors.

- **R&D.** PWS will constantly improve its Web site, but the outsourced vendors will provide all R&D efforts. PWS has chosen its vendors both by their ability to deliver quality service today and by their ability to keep ahead of service competitors in the future.

- **Marketing.** Marketing and sales expenses are expected to be 10% of sales. This is lower than the more typical 20% because of the use of students in networking and mentoring relationships with potential and actual clients.

Balance sheet assumptions are often omitted from a plan. That's a mistake, because they are an ideal summary tool for highlighting the strong points of a business concept. The PWS example quickly highlights its high margins and low marketing costs in its assumptions. I personally like to read balance sheet assumptions first, because they give the gist of whether or not a company will be profitable.

*T*his use of proceeds is more detailed than usual. Typically, plans will break out use of proceeds only into broad categories such as marketing, legal expenses, salaries, and production start-up. This detail is useful in this plan because of the age of the entrepreneurs. The detail shows they have thought their plan through and that they are cautious with money.

- **General and Administrative.** Projected at 8% of sales due to the use of student interns for accounting and the comparatively low salaries of the company's executives.
- **Accounts Receivable.** PWS terms are payable in 60 days, but financial forecasts use a more realistic 45-day payment cycle.
- **Accounts Payable.** 30 days after the receipt of the invoice.

Funding Request

PWS is looking to raise $60,000 for the year starting on September 1, 2001 to cover operating costs. We currently have 160 shares of stock valued at $1000 per share. Based on the valuation of $160,000, an investment of $60,000 would be a 37.5% share of the company, or 60 shares.

Use of Funds (continued on next page)

Item	Cost ($)
Intranet	240
Toll-Free Voice and Fax Service	240
Web Hosting (co-location in future)	300
Domain Name	35
Software (ACT, Office, Flash, Photoshop, DW QuickB)	1,000
Mailbox Rental	180
Public Relations Specialist	3,000
Lawyer (incorporation, documents)	2,000
Accountant (quarterly, taxes)	1,000
Equipment (cell phone, laptop, PDA, LCD projector)	4,000

Item	Cost ($)
Office Supplies	300
Laptop and Cell Phone Access	600
Magazine and Trade Publication Subscriptions	300
Promotional Materials (press kit, sales pitch, business cards, brochure, client gifts, thank-you cards)	4,500
Networking (BNI, MCC, AIP, Events, Fat Thursday, Conferences)	3,000
Search Engine Advertising	2,000
Web Development RFP Exchanges and Lists	5,000
Miscellaneous	4,000
Salaries	30,000
Total	61,695

Exit Strategy

The company is planning either an IPO or a merger with or sale to a larger Internet consulting firm in three to four years.

THE BUSINESS
PLAN
SAMPLE
PLANS

INTERNET COMPANY BUSINESS PLAN

SanaSana

Executive Summary

Business Description

SanaSana comprises a B2B2C solution that provides an efficient, mutually beneficial partnership between Hispanic consumers of health care and the businesses—payers, providers, and suppliers of health services and non-health-related companies alike—that would like to serve them. Once established in the U.S., SanaSana will expand abroad, where native Spanish speakers desire access to medical knowledge.

Target Customers

SanaSana's target customers, which SanaSana calls "business partners," are the companies that want access to the Hispanic audience that is coming to the Web site. By working with SanaSana, business partners benefit from increased access to a growing population that will come to regard SanaSana as its most trusted source of health-related information. This target audience is otherwise hard to reach cost-effectively, as in most of the U.S. Hispanics make up a minority percentage of the population.

Currently there are approximately 10 million Hispanic households in the U.S. and about 35% of those households have Internet access. This is a large relatively affluent market that needs and wants additional health care information, especially relating to medical problems that affect Hispanics more than the general population.

Management Team

Combined, the founders have over 50 years of direct experience in general management, e-commerce, finance, marketing, medicine, and operations.

M. Elizabeth Barton, Customer Experience. Ms. Barton brings accomplishments from such companies as Booz Allen & Hamilton and The Procter & Gamble Co., with expertise in consulting, finance, marketing, and technology.

Carlos R. De Jesus, Marketing. Mr. De Jesus boasts a history of achievement in marketing, operations, and management at Frito Lay, Co. In addition, he recently led the development and execution at The Procter & Gamble Co. of an e-commerce program.

Adam W. Farkas, M.D., Technology. Dr. Farkas founded his own dial-up Internet service and led the American Medical Student Association Task Force on Computers in Medicine. Most recently, he formulated on behalf of Cerner Corporation a strategic plan for a line of Internet-based consumer health care software products.

Ricardo Fernandez, Business Development. Mr. Fernandez managed financial analysis and reporting for the e-commerce department at Citibank Universal Card Services. In addition, he recently helped KeyBank U.S.A. realize $2 million in annual savings through improved processes in its loan operations.

Financial Projections

Figure 15-1 shows financial projections for five years.

	Start-up	Year 1	Year 2	Year 3	Year 4	Year 5
Revenues	0	7,200	13,984	23,307	38,399	61,569
Expenses	1,922	16,044	15,514	21,206	27,976	36,866
EBT	(1,922)	(8,844)	(1,529)	2,101	10,423	24,703

All numbers in thousands

FIGURE 15-1. Five-year financial projections

Financing Plan

In order to launch SanaSana, we are seeking a first round investment of $2 million through the sale of stock, which will allow SanaSana to continue through the first four months of operations. Two potential exit strategies exist for the investor: an initial public offering or an acquisition merger with a private or public company.

1.0 Business Overview

1.1 SanaSana Vision Statement

We envision developing our consumers into informed, proactive users of health services. They will be empowered by current, customized information, products and services that our industry partners present. In turn, our industry partners will have opportunities to reach critical new markets through novel business relationships that reduce associated costs and increase potential revenues.

1.2 Background

SanaSana's business concept is the result of its founders' desire to provide health care information for non-physician Hispanics. The management team includes both a Hispanic physician and Hispanic users of medical care and they understand both the needs of the market and the lack of information available to them. Currently there exists little health information translated for Hispanics and written for non-physicians. SanaSana's library of understandable, Spanish-language health information and novel, proprietary HealthCapsules™ represent a vital resource for the Hispanic community.

1.3 Key Features

For Hispanic Consumers

- **Off- and online community,** which features personalized e-mail responders, support groups, chat rooms, and partnerships with community groups—such as those in churches, hospitals, and libraries.
- **HealthCapsules™,** which provide customizable updates via our proprietary e-mail newsletters.
- **Referrals,** which report consumer recommendations on health care products and services.
- **Privacy protection,** which we consider the cornerstone of a viable relationship among our partners.

For Business Partners

- **Online market research,** which improves our partners' understanding of Hispanics' preferences.
- **New product introduction tools,** which facilitate our partners' launches of new products.
- **Office and practice management applications referrals,** to allow outsourcing of non-medical-related tasks to fellow alliance partners to enhance revenue and reduce costs.
- **Web hosting services,** which offer hosting of Web pages with online scheduling for physician partners.

1.4 Market Test Results

Between August and December 1999, the team conducted 64 interviews and surveys with consumers and physicians. We also met with more than 22 representatives from pharmaceutical, consumer products, hospitals, and insurance companies to obtain feedback and gauge interest on our idea. The results of this primary research support our initial hypothesis for the merits of this business concept. All results signal a strong need for our products and services across our target Hispanic consumers and our industry partners.

Key insights from consumers, physicians, medical teaching institutions, pharmaceutical and consumer product companies:

- **Consumers:** Consumers crave personalized health information, preferably in their native language.
- **Physicians:** Hispanics are less educated about health and less medically studied than typical patients.
- **Medical teaching institutions:** There is a general lack of quality health information provided in Spanish, and they would be willing to pay for access to such information.
- **Drug company representatives:** Due to the growing Hispanic and Latino populations, drug companies desire access to this demographic for participation in clinical trials.
- **Consumer product brand managers:** Future growth opportunities in consumer products exist through the creation of separate products for the health-conscious consumer and especially the Hispanic consumer.

1.5 Current Status

SanaSana is in the process of raising money to start operations. An initial operating plan and an initial round of industry contacts have been made. The company anticipates it can be operating four months after receiving financing.

1.6 Future Plans

With initial success in the U.S., we will then expand internationally. Our extraordinary opportunities for expansion come from three key areas:

- Leveraging the reputation and relationships from a successful U.S. launch.
- Launching SanaSana in Latin America and Spanish-speaking countries elsewhere.
- Scaling the SanaSana "information-transformation engine" into non-Spanish-speaking countries.

2.0 Target Customers and Markets

2.1 Hispanic and Latino Consumers

Two primary market phenomena make this consumer segment attractive to SanaSana:

- *Hispanics and Latinos represent the fastest-growing segment in the United States.* With over 2% annual growth for decades to come, the size of the segment will surpass that of all other ethnic groups combined by the year 2020. In addition, nearly 50% of Hispanic and Latino households are projected to have Internet access by the year 2005.

Growth Trends for Hispanics and Latinos in the U.S.

- *Hispanics and Latinos increasingly turn to the Internet for health information.* Over 17 million U.S. adults have searched the Internet for health information. This number will surpass 30 million by year-end. Of these, over 15% are ethnic minorities (see Figure 15-2).

	1999	2001	2003	2005
Total U.S. Population	272,888	277,800	282,800	287,700
Total U.S. Hispanics	32,000	34,700	35,900	38,200
Total U.S. Hispanics Online	3,541	6,445	8,379	14,160
Total U.S. Hispanic Households	9,200	9,600	9,900	10,300
With Internet Access	16.6%	24.0%	34.3%	49.5%

Figures in thousands
Source: *Falling Through the Net: Defining the Digital Divide* , U.S. Department of Commerce, July 1999

FIGURE 15-2. Hispanic market trends

- *The Hispanic health indices differ from others.* For instance, Hispanics suffer more from emphysema, hepatitis, hypertension, infant mortality, and teen pregnancy. As a whole, Hispanics desire more health information, products, and services from payers, providers and suppliers of health information, products, and services.

- *Hispanics are becoming more technologically savvy, and the need for Hispanic-specific information is expanding.*

2.2 Business Partners

SanaSana's target business partner customers are providers of health- and non-health-related products and services that focus part or all of their marketing efforts on the Hispanic community. Among potential business partners, four alone (drug companies, hospitals, physicians, and medical equipment suppliers) enjoyed combined revenues of over $715 billion. Some of the target customers are:

- *Third-party payers of health services*—like insurance companies and the U.S. government—spent extraordinary amounts for health care reimbursements.

These payers continually search for more efficient ways to decrease the amount of unnecessary care through consumer education.

- *Hispanic and Latino purchasing power is higher than ever.* Purchasing power is $400 billion in 2000. Hispanic buying power has grown over 67% since 1990. In 1998, advertisers spent more that $2 billion trying to reach consumers of Hispanic descent.

- *Providers of health care*—such as hospitals and pharmacies—have marketing and sales budgets to attract new customers for their services.

- *Suppliers of health services*—from academic medical institutions to medical equipment companies—also will pay for access to SanaSana's consumers. The pharmaceutical industry alone will spend an estimated $1.5 billion in 1999 on untargeted direct-to-consumer marketing.

- *Non-health services suppliers*—like consumer products companies—offer more and more "healthy living" products, such as allergy control cleaners and "heart smart" foods. The companies also appreciate the opportunity to perform focus groups and test their products with SanaSana consumers.

Many companies are trying to understand and reach the Hispanic population; they try new packaging, products, and organizational structures to better meet Hispanics' needs. The challenge going forward is to find innovative ways by which to communicate with this crucial consumer group.

2.3 Market Size

Hispanics and Latinos represent the fastest growing segment in the United States. With over 2% annual growth for decades to come, the size of the segment will surpass that of all other ethnic groups combined by the year 2020. In addition, nearly 50% of Hispanic and Latino households are projected to have Internet access by the year 2005 (see Figure 15-2).

2.4 Competition

Despite the growing number of Spanish-language medical sites, the quality and breadth of information remains limited. While all pose potential threats, they leave gaps in the competitive landscape. No competitor focuses on being the single source of health information for the Spanish speaker. SanaSana will be the only bilingual, customized health information destination that supports interactive community activities and makes the issues of the Hispanic and Latino health care consumer its top priority.

Competitors	Players	Competitive Checklist	
General Spanish-language portals All-purpose sites providing search engine with links to potentially thousands of other sites	Ole! QuePasa StarMedia Yupi	Threat	High
		Focus	Non-medical
		Capitalization	High
		Alliances	High
		Hispanic Focus	High
		Reliability/Quality	High
English-language health portals Content providers serving as stand-alone entities with news, community, interactive applications, and medical advice from professionals	DrKoop OnHealth webMD	Threat	High
		Focus	Medical
		Capitalization	High
		Alliances	High
		Hispanic Focus	Low
		Reliability/Quality	High

FIGURE 15-3. Review of competitors (continued on next page)

Competitors	Players	Competitive Checklist	
Spanish-language health portals Sites with links to Spanish-language health sites worldwide; focused on health and targeted toward Spanish-speaking consumers	Vistalink MedicinaTV MiPediatrica GINEweb Salud	Threat	High
		Focus	Medical
		Capitalization	Low/Medium
		Alliances	Low
		Hispanic Focus	High
		Reliability/Quality	Medium
Insurance and managed care Sites serving primarily as advertising tool with expected transition to information source for members	Aetna Allstate Prudential	Threat	Low/Medium
		Focus	Advertising
		Capitalization	High
		Alliances	Medium
		Hispanic Focus	Low
		Reliability/Quality	High
Governmental organizations Usually static text files with links to government-generated health information for consumers	Healthfinder	Threat	Low
		Focus	Medical
		Capitalization	Medium
		Alliances	Low
		Hispanic Focus	Low
		Reliability/Quality	High
Private Content/Physicians Content developed by private citizens and physicians in solo or small group practices	Private citizens Solo practices Small groups	Threat	Low
		Focus	Solely Medical
		Capitalization	Low
		Alliances	Low
		Hispanic Focus	High
		Reliability/Quality	Low

FIGURE 15-3. Review of competitors (continued)

3.0 Products

3.1 Consumers

The Web site and its services are all free to the consumer.

3.2 Business Partners

3.2.1 Advertising-Related Products

- **Banner Advertising.** This will be a typical banner advertising program, with banners available for the main site, site categories, and site search terms. Advertising will be sold on a cost-per-thousand basis.
- **HealthCapsules™.** HealthCapsules are e-mailed to consumers on topics in which they have already expressed an interest. HealthCapsules will provide information from industry partners related to the topic. Partners can either purchase an individual page in a HealthCapsule or furnish the entire Health-Capsule on a cost per thousand.
- **Referral network.** Health providers are listed on the site by geographic area. Consumers can also do a search for health providers in their area. Listing in the referral network is free, but enhanced listing with additional information or an ad has additional costs.
- **Site sponsorship and targeted advertising.** We will build long-term agreements with business partners by offering them the opportunity to sponsor our key content areas and display information to our registered users. Our staff will screen all information before final release.

3.2.2 Online Research and New Product Management Tools

- **Online market research services.** We will provide online focus group and survey services to improve our partners' understanding of these different groups. Again, as a portal destination site for health care,

SUCCESSFUL BUSINESS MODELS

SanaSana will be able to find consumers fitting a certain profile for its business partners for online surveys.

- **New product management tools.** To facilitate our partners' launches of new products, SanaSana will provide a space by which to communicate new product news. We will also serve as an intermediary for new product sampling programs and consumer feedback.
- **Clinical trial participant referral.** Through the registration process, consumers can opt-into clinical trials for new drugs and treatment regiments. We will match interested, appropriate consumers with relevant, well-designed studies.

3.2.3 Office and Practice Management Referral Network

- **Office and practice management applications.** SanaSana will offer application service provision (ASP). To our provider partners, we will provide use of office management tools and services. Other partners will be able to sell such services to our wide network of member physicians and hospitals.

3.2.4 Web Hosting Services

To facilitate and attract new physician partners, we will offer to host their practices' Web pages. Some capabilities we would include are online scheduling and children's inoculation reminder service.

3.3 Consumer Benefits

Our company's success stems from its ability to offer personalized, accurate information while protecting our users' confidentiality, thereby providing a convenient, trustworthy way to become informed and proactive about health. We offer:

206 / CHAPTER 15

- **Off- and online community.** We will partner with established community organizations to help educate Hispanics on their health and on the use of technology. For our online users, we will offer virtual support groups, chat rooms, and e-mail chains.

- **Tailored portal.** Our site will offer the traditional portal-type services like bulletin boards and searchable databases. Our differentiation comes from the ease of personalization and streamlined access to data. Through the registration process, consumers can personalize their news briefs, product updates, and HealthCapsules™.

- **HealthCapsules™.** The HealthCapsule™, SanaSana's customized bilingual e-mail newsletter, is our way of keeping SanaSana's registered users up-to-date in their topics of interest. The information of interest to each SanaSana user will be summarized and sent to the user's secure SanaSana mailbox with user-specified timing (default timing is weekly) and format.

- **Referrals.** Our rating system asks consumers to report their health-care-related experiences by recording their answers to the crucial question: "Would you recommend this product (or physician, hospital, procedure, insurance company, medication, etc.) to a friend or relative?"

- **Physician interaction.** Site users can correspond directly with their personal physicians (also registered site users), thereby increasing preventative health practices. Additionally, our staff doctors will be available to answer questions in Spanish or English via e-mail and chat rooms. We will also have a physician go "live on the Net" to answer questions, creating a human image users can relate to.

- **Privacy protection.** We understand that protecting the privacy of our users' information maximizes the trust necessary to build relationships in this space. Our site enables consumers to establish pseudonyms, complete with an accompanying Web-based e-mail address hosted by SanaSana. By encouraging this high degree of anonymity and privacy protection, people will feel safe surfing our site for their health care needs without fear of releasing privileged or personal information.

3.4 Business Partner Benefits

By working with SanaSana, all of our industry partners—both health and non-health service companies—will benefit from increased access to a crucial population that will come to regard SanaSana as its most trusted source of health-related information. The benefits to each of our major business partners is shown in Figure 15-4.

Payers	Providers	Suppliers
Governmental Agencies and Insurance Companies • Reduction in unnecessary care • Increases in plan enrollees	Hospital Systems and Physicians • Application Service Provision • Inclusion in referral database • Complimentary Web hosting with e-mail address	Medical Device, Pharmaceutical, and Consumer Goods Companies • Access to clinical trial participants • Opportunities for targeted marketing and sampling campaigns • New product pages

FIGURE 15-4. Benefits to business partners

3.5 Initial Content Strategy

In order to provide consumer health information, SanaSana must form broad alliances.

- **Partnerships with key Hispanic doctors.** The trusting relationship between physicians and patients comprises an essential ingredient for optimal medical care. To this end, SanaSana will identify and align itself closely with leading Spanish-speaking physicians in core cities. Having these doctors endorse and critique our service will allow us to provide a uniquely valuable product to Hispanic health consumers.

- **Alliance with key medical institutions.** Several medical institutions and societies specifically serve the Hispanic community. Professional organizations, like the National Hispanic Medical Association (NHMA) and the Association of Hispanic Nurses, can help us to establish deep community ties and enhance our credibility. We are currently discussing alliance opportunities with the NHMA.

- **Alliance with existing Internet vehicles.** Several large Spanish-language portals offer links to Spanish-language medical sites, but these sites lack consistent quality and reliable usefulness. Because of their large user base, portals like Yupi and Starmedia represent important alliance partners for SanaSana, allowing rapid capture of a high proportion of Hispanics online.

3.6 Design and Development of Future Products and Services

Proprietary content development. Our desire to provide information of the highest quality will require the initial content synopses be generated by physicians. We will utilize a network of semi-retired physicians, resident physicians, and practicing physicians for this content development.

Additionally, three physicians on staff will function as gate-keepers for the recommended articles. The editorial staff will initially consist of 46 people.

Content acquisition. Content that the SanaSana site will deliver to consumers and its associated partners will initially be derived from medical journals, peer-reviewed research, news releases, and other health-related communications. Much of the content, such as general background on afflictions, photos, or drug interactions already exists in databases and can be accessed for a fee. Novel content will be generated internally. Each user page of content will be created dynamically, applying user-defined selections.

Translation logistics. An editorial staff will carry out both editing and translation. We will outsource this service to bilingual technical writers that take the physicians' summaries of prominent articles and then translate them into Spanish.

4.0 Marketing

4.1 Objectives

SanaSana's goal is to become far and away the leader in providing health care information to the Hispanic community. It expects to grow rapidly to meet consumer and business partner demand. Figure 15-5 shows the growth of the user base.

4.2 Positioning Strategy

SanaSana positioning strategy is designed to both position it as the market leaders and to provide significant barriers to entry to future competition. SanaSana's competitive advantage lies in two areas:

- **Content.** There exists little health information trans-

	Startup	Year 1	Year 2	Year 3	Year 4	Year 5
Total U.S. Hispanics Online	3,541	4,958	6,445	8,379	10,892	14,160
Registered SanaSana Users	NA	198	258	335	436	566
Acquisition Cost per New User	NA	$40	$50	$55	$60	$65

FIGURE 15-5. User base growth

lated for Hispanics and written for non-physicians. Thus, SanaSana's library of understandable, Spanish-language health information and novel, proprietary HealthCapsules™ represents a barrier to entry and revenue potential.

- **Community.** In order to ensure success, SanaSana must create a vibrant community of medical institutions, prominent Hispanic doctors, technology, and Hispanic consumers. Once established, these relationships and this community will serve as potent barriers to entry. Because of first-mover advantage and our contacts within medical institutions and others in the industry, we are well positioned to create this barrier. (Figure 15-6 shows the barriers to entry we are developing.)

Community	Content
Prominent, concerned physicians	Proprietary, novel HealthCapsules™
Community based computer terminals	Consistently current, reliably accurate
Physician office presence	Easily understandable and useful
Industry relationships and contacts	English, Spanish, and Portuguese

FIGURE 15-6. Barriers to entry

4.3 Marketing Plan

The marketing plan focuses upon actions that will occur during the short term to create barriers to entry, ensure sources of revenue, secure customers for the site, create trust in the Hispanic community, and generate grassroots excitement for SanaSana.

The marketing program in Phases 3 and 4 continues to generate visitors for SanaSana while establishing brand awareness and equity for both consumers and business partners.

		Secure Alliances and Partnerships	Marketing Vehicle Employed
Phase 1 May thru July 2000	B2C	Community service organizations in Los Angeles, New York, and Miami • Hispanic Business Association • Parents as Teachers	• Trips to target cities • E-mail • Letters • Phone calls • Personal contacts • Site demonstrations
	B2B	National Hispanic Medical Association Consumer Goods Companies • Procter & Gamble • General Mills • S.C. Johnson	• Personal contacts • Letters • E-mail • Phone calls
Phase 2 Aug thru Sept 2000	B2C	Community service organizations in San Francisco, Chicago, and Houston • Hispanic Business Association • Parents as Teachers	• Trips to target cities • E-mail • Letters • Phone calls • Personal contacts • Site demonstrations
	B2B	Insurance Companies • Allstate Doctors in Los Angeles, New York, and Miami Pharmaceutical Companies • Perrigo • Warner Lambert	• Trips to business partners • Personal contacts • Letters • E-mail • Phone calls

FIGURE 15-7. Marketing plan highlights (continued on next page)

		Secure Alliances and Partnerships	Marketing Vehicle Employed
Phase 3 Oct thru Dec 2000	B2C	Government Agencies • HUD $$ • Health Community service organizations in San Antonio, Dallas, and Albuquerque • Hispanic Business Association • Parents as Teachers	• Trips to target cities • Public relations • Advertising in 9 cities • TV (Univision, Telemundo) • Radio • Newspaper
	B2B	Doctors in San Francisco, Chicago, and Houston Medical Supply Vendors Hispanic Advertisers • Sears • AT&T • GM • McDonald's	• Written correspondence • Trips to target cities • Articles in NHMA newsletter and Hispanic Business Times • Computers in doctor offices in Los Angeles, New York, and Miami
Phase 4 Jan thru Mar 2001	B2C	Community service organizations in Brownsville, Phoenix, El Paso, San Diego, and Fresno On the Ground in LA, New York, and Miami	• Trips to target cities • Public relations • Community health lectures • Advertising in all cities • TV (Univision, Telemundo) • Radio • Newspaper
	B2B	Doctors in remaining cities Logical Web Sites • Yupi • Gloria Estefan, Edward James Olmos Newspapers Medical supply vendors	• Written correspondence • Trips to target cities • Links on partner Web sites • Computers in doctor offices in San Francisco, Chicago, and Houston

FIGURE 15-7. Marketing plan highlights (continued)

4.4 Initial Pricing Strategy

Partial funding for the marketing and operation activities of SanaSana will come from our industry partners. SanaSana's initial pricing strategy was generated using competitors' pricing models as a benchmark (see Figure 15-8).

Banner Advertising (CPM)	$35
HealthCapsules (CPM)	$45
Content Area Sponsorship Fee	$120,000
Online Focus Groups Set-up Fee	$2,000
Online Focus Groups Fee (10 participants)	$2,000
Online Surveys (1,000 distributed)	$30,000
Sample Fee (CPM)	$200

FIGURE 15-8. Product pricing

5.0 Management

Combined, the seven founders have over 50 years of direct experience in general management, e-commerce, finance, marketing, medicine, and operations. The roles of each team member are in line with qualifications and interests, bolstering the feasibility of our plans. Figure 15-9 shows the background of each member and the organization of SanaSana.

Note: The writers of this plan provided detailed résumés in their Appendix.

	Background	SanaSana Role
Elizabeth Barton	Sales, Consulting	Customer Experience
Carlos De Jesus	Sales, Brand Management	Marketing
Adam Farkas, M.D.	Medicine, E-commerce	Technology
Ricardo Fernandez	Finance, Brand Management	Business Development
Brian Khoury	Finance, Entrepreneur	Communications
Hyung Kim, M.D.	Medicine, Academic Professor	Medical Affairs
Jamel Richardson	Operations, Brand Management	Operations

FIGURE 15-9. Team member matrix

6.0 Operations

6.1 System Design

While technology changes rapidly, our operation team's goal remains constant: to create a compelling environment for our customers. To achieve this, our technological solution must provide a high degree of reliability and scalability. A summary of the architecture that powers the site is outlined below.

- **System architecture.** The Sanasana.com Web site will be built atop the arsDigita Community System (ACS) platform. This powerful open-source toolkit is used to build interactive Web-based applications. It runs on a variety of UNIX-platforms and interfaces with Oracle 8.1 RDBMS and AOLServer to produce highly scalable, reliable, and portable database-backed Web solutions.

- **Development hardware.** Our choice of software platform allows us to use a network of Intel-based workstations running FreeBSD UNIX as our development environment. These machines provide us with a fully functional test environment from which our software and content can be directly uploaded to a production environment.

- **Production hardware/connectivity.** For a maximal degree of reliability and scalability, we will use Sun 450 Enterprise-class machines in our production environment. These machines will be physically co-located at above.net in Vienna, Virginia. This allows us to leverage above.net's expertise in system administration and physical protection for mission-critical servers. It also provides us with a mechanism to transparently increase our bandwidth to the Internet as our user base grows, preventing system slowdowns and unnecessary downtime.

7.0 Financial Projections

The financial projections for SanaSana are quite encouraging. The growth of Hispanic adoption of Internet usage, the lack of useful health content targeted at the Hispanic/Latino population, and the opportunity for product developers to seek feedback from a targeted community in a cost-effective manner provide a unique, yet short window of opportunity for SanaSana to be a first mover. The following sections provide a synopsis of the financial outlook for the business.

7.1 Five-Year Financial Summary

Figure 15-10 summarizes operating earnings for the first five years.

	Start-up	Year 1	Year 2	Year 3	Year 4	Year 5
Revenue						
Sponsorships	0	1,440	3,840	7,560	13,920	23,400
Product Development Services	0	3,663	5,598	8,192	12,267	17,808
Research Studies and Commerce	0	1,265	2,619	4,455	7,201	12,237
Advertising	0	832	1,927	3,101	5,011	8,125
Total Revenues	0	7,200	13,984	23,307	38,399	61,569
Expenses						
Content Development	406	372	1,224	2,322	3,526	5,044
Operations	231	1,203	1,444	1,788	2,177	2,716
Marketing	220	12,110	10,129	14,018	18,777	25,129
G&A	1,065	2,359	2,716	3,078	3,496	3,977
Total Expenses	1,922	16,044	15,514	21,206	27,976	36,866

FIGURE 15-10. Summary of operating earnings, first five years (continued on next page)

	Start-up	Year 1	Year 2	Year 3	Year 4	Year 5
EBT	(1,922)	(8,844)	(1,529)	2,101	10,423	24,703
Inflated EBT (3%/Year)	(1,922)	(9,110)	(1,622)	2,296	11,731	28,637
Taxes (assumes 35% tax rate)	(673)	(3,188)	(568)	804	4,106	10,023
Net Earnings	(1,249)	(5,921)	(1,055)	1,493	7,625	18,614
Cash Flow (adj for tax credits)	(1,922)	(9,110)	(1,622)	5,922	7,625	18,614
Cumulative Cash Flow	(1,922)	(11,032)	(12,654)	(6,733)	893	19,507

FIGURE 15-10. Summary of operating earnings (continued)

7.2 Assumptions

This income model is contingent upon a number of key volume estimates. Figure 15-11 provides the more critical volume assumptions for SanaSana.

	Start-up	Year 1	Year 2	Year 3	Year 4	Year 5
# Hispanics in the U.S. online	3,541,333	4,957,867	6,445,227	8,378,795	10,892,433	14,160,163
# registered users		198,315	257,809	335,152	435,697	566,407
# content areas		20	40	60	80	100
# e-mails sent		12,606,045	26,090,278	37,309,097	53,352,009	76,293,372
# HealthCapsules™ sent per year per content area		52	52	52	52	52
Total new product space purchased per year		480	960	1,440	1,920	2,400
Licensing agreements (content liscensing)		6	9	15	20	30
# willing to participate in research studies		618	4,561	5,930	7,708	10,021

FIGURE 15-11. Critical volume assumptions for SanaSana (continued on the next page)

	Start-up	Year 1	Year 2	Year 3	Year 4	Year 5
# new product samples sent per year		1,189,888	1,703,098	2,440,058	3,513,416	5,058,613
# surveys distributed per year		98,166	127,732	166,368	217,774	285,046
# focus groups per year		90	150	210	285	360

FIGURE 15-11. Critical volume assumptions for SanaSana (continued)

7.3 Funding Requirements

Figure 15-12 shows the amount and timing for funds.

	EOP Start-up	EOP Year 1	EOP Year 2	EOP Year 3	EOP Year 4	EOP Year 5
Cash Flows from Operations						
Net Earnings	(1,249,308)	(5,748,894)	(993,987)	1,365,954	6,775,079	16,056,896
Change in Working Capital						
Decrease (Increase) Accounts Receivable	0	(1,374,509)	(1,305,680)	(1,730,704)	(2,814,255)	(4,348,203)
Decrease (Increase) Inventory	(22,077)	2,000	(16,392)	(21,099)	(23,162)	(29,190)
Decrease (Increase) Prepaid Expenses	(8,400)	(1,600)	(4,000)	0	0	0
Increase (Decrease) Accounts Payable	219,135	975,781	(46,051)	444,257	529,446	700,868
Total Cash from Operations	(1,060,650)	(6,147,222)	(2,366,110)	58,408	4,467,108	12,380,362
Cash Flow from Investing						
Investments	0	0	0	0	0	0
Total Cash from Investing	0	0	0	0	0	0

FIGURE 15-12. Pro forma statement of cash flows (FY 2000) (continued on next page)

	EOP Start-up	EOP Year 1	EOP Year 2	EOP Year 3	EOP Year 4	EOP Year 5
Cash Flow from Financing						
Short-Term Debt	0	0	0	0	0	0
Long-Term Debt	0	0	0	0	0	0
Owners' Equity	2,000,000	6,000,000	2,000,000	0	0	0
Total Cash from Financing	2,000,000	6,000,000	2,000,000	0	0	0
Net Increase (Decrease) in Cash	939,350	(147,212)	(366,110)	58,408	4,467,108	12,380,362
Cash, Beginning of Period	0	939,350	792,128	426,019	484,426	4,951,535
Cash, End of Period	939,350	792,128	426,019	484,426	4,951,535	17,331,896

FIGURE 15-12. Pro forma statement of cash flows (FY 2000) (continued)

7.4 Use of Funds

- **Start-up (June 2000 to December 2000).** During the first six months after launch (start-up phase), SanaSana will invest a majority of its capital in building the Web site and content for its business. Also, SanaSana will begin a communication and sales effort with potential business partners and doctors. The goal of this effort is to have a set of established businesses and medical professionals supporting the business prior to its launch. A smaller set of funds will also be used to begin a marketing effort to potential Hispanic users.
- **Year 1 (December 2000 to December 2001).** The majority of the funds available in this phase will be spent on consumer marketing. As described above, the success of this business is dependent upon achieving a critical mass of consumers. It is only with

this large, targeted consumer-base that SanaSana can expect to earn revenue from advertising.

7.5 Long-Term Financial Strategy

We see two options for our future financial strategy: internal expansion or exit strategy.

7.5.1 Expansion Model

In order to increase market share and access additional markets through expansion, SanaSana must raise additional capital.

- **Venture capital.** SanaSana seeks to partner with venture capital industry leaders that would provide both financial assistance as well as industry, legal, technological, and marketing insights. We foresee at least two rounds of VC infusion prior to an IPO.
- **IPO and secondary IPO.** An IPO would clearly benefit the company by allowing us to leverage the additional resources and market valuation to purchase additional information and increase company credibility. The additional funds, similar to the VC expansion model, would be utilized to increase promotion and acquire a stronger market presence. A successful secondary IPO will again allow the company to raise "cheap" capital to promote expansion into new markets where publicly traded shares may not be suitable.
- **Franchising.** A clear competitive advantage of SanaSana is our rapid information translation model. The success of this model will translate with ease throughout other countries.
- **Partnerships.** Currently we are seeking partnerships with traditional media, newspapers, and television networks, fueling expansion by infusing capital and offering cross-marketing opportunities.

7.5.2 Acquisition Model

Current competitors in both the Spanish-language and English-language market space are obviously acquiring candidates.

- **English-language-based health sites.** We foresee an opportunity to be purchased by organizations seeking to enter our space, such as webMD, Medscape, or drkoop. This would allow the English-language-based competitors to quickly gain users, realize synergies, and address the growth needs that have been worked into their forecasts.

- **Spanish-based Internet businesses.** Again, we believe that there will ultimately be a consolidation in the industry in the next two to four years. As the Spanish-based Internet market continues to grow, there will also be a need to establish credibility and gain users.

- **New entry.** The Internet business is still in its infancy in the Spanish market. Subsequently, there will be companies seeking to enter this space. A quick way to gain credibility would be to purchase a successful site that has a transferable business model.

# CHAPTER 16

RETAIL STORE BUSINESS PLAN

THE BOULDER SHOP

This plan was prepared by Luke and Lisa Walsh, owners of The Boulder Stop in Boulder, Colorado and Doug Wilson, Palo Alto Software, www.paloalto.com, 800-229-7526.

Note: Certain parts of this plan refer to specific competitors and vendors. The writer of the plan didn't wish some of these companies to be identified and the word "[Omitted]" is substituted for the companies' names in this plan. All of the other information is still present.

1.0 Executive Summary

- The Boulder Stop is a store that will offer high-end rock climbing gear and classic Northwest coffee. We will purchase the gear wholesale and have it shipped via FedEx and UPS, both of which serve the Bend/Redmond business community. We will buy our freshly roasted coffee beans from Espresso Harvest, a Bend area distributor and reseller of gourmet coffee beans.

- The store is located one mile from Smith Rock State Park in the Central Oregon desert. It is conveniently located in an area frequented by national and international tourists.

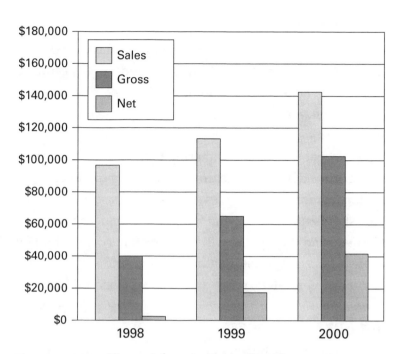

FIGURE 16-1. Financial projections, first three years

1.1 Objectives

1. To make The Boulder Stop a local favorite for tourists, hikers, and climbers on their way to/from Smith Rock.
2. To achieve the largest market share in the region for rock-climbing gear.
3. To be an active and vocal member of the community, sponsoring five or more events during the year, including fun climbs, family bouldering, and celebrity-hosted competitions.
4. To achieve a 65% gross margin within the first year. Our conservative projected gross margin is 45%.
5. To achieve a net profit of $30,000 by year two.

1.2 Mission

The Boulder Stop is an equipment store and cafe specializing in premium rock-climbing gear and coffee/espresso drinks. We believe rock climbing should be safe and fun. We understand that rock climbers need a healthy dose of the newest gear, fresh snacks, and raw caffeine.

Our goal is to be the gathering points for rock climbers living in and visiting Central Oregon. Smith Rock State Park is one of the finest rock-climbing parks in the world. Our staff is fluent in several languages, including Spanish, German, and French. We will be the region's destination for those who want to know all there is to know about rock-climbing gear, safety, rules, and events in Central Oregon.

1.3 Keys to Success

To succeed in this business we must:
- Sell products that are of the highest reliability and quality. We must offer as many or more premium products than REI offers online and through its Eugene and Portland stores.
- Provide for the satisfaction of 100% of our customers and vendors.
- Be an active member of the community: i.e., host sport-climbing and rock-climbing events.
- Negotiate valuable contracts with great distributors such as Trago, Petzl, Black Diamond, Beal, Ushba Mountain Works, and others.

1.4 Funding Sought

The purpose of this business plan is to secure a $11,700 Small Business Administration (SBA) loan.

2.0 Company Summary

The Boulder Stop is a store that sells premium coffee and gear. The cafe is located one mile from Smith Rock State Park in Central Oregon.

The Boulder Stop was incorporated in the State of Oregon on January 1, 1997. It is privately held and managed by Luke Walsh. The company has established a central office at 1455 Portland St., Bend, OR 97701. This location is designed for purchasing, storage, and contract negotiations. Service purchases will be forwarded to this office for review and approval. All purchase order authorizations will also be approved at this office.

2.1 Company Ownership

The Boulder Stop is a privately held corporation. Luke Walsh owns 60% of The Boulder Stop; his wife Lisa owns 40%. This company operates under the jurisdiction of the State of Oregon and the United States of America as an S Corporation. If the company shows steady or exponential growth, the owners will prepare the company for re-establishment as a C corporation. At the moment, the owners wish to benefit from the single taxation of an S corporation.

2.2 Start-up Summary

Our incorporation costs are listed below, as well as the cost of retaining a marketing consultant to manage local impact-management teams and to issue a community impact report to major public and private agencies within the region. They will also inform The Boulder Stop owners about how to effectively communicate with the community leaders to get approval for opening the store. Our lawyer will be responsible for preempting any local government conflicts having to do with zoning and/or permit allowance.

There will be other normal business costs, such as a $1,000,000 liability umbrella, rent, interior design costs, and opening day promotions.

The largest equipment purchase will be that of a Conti brand commercial espresso machine. This machine, named "The TwinStar," comes with an 18-month warranty on parts and a 12-month warranty on labor. These espresso machines are world-renowned for their high quality and performance features. The company will start with two months' inventory on hand. The majority of company assets will reside in inventory. The starting cash balance will be $3,000.

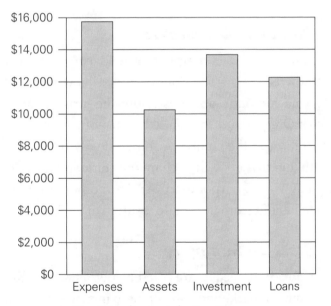

FIGURE 16-2. Start-up financial situation

Start-up Expenses	Amount
Legal	$300
Marketing consultant	$4,500
Business and liability insurance	$600
1st month's payment amount + deposit	$2,500
Design costs	$3,500
First-week promotion	$1,100
Expensed equipment	$3,500
Other	$0
Total Start-up Expenses	**$16,000**

Start-up Assets Needed	Amount
Cash requirements	$3,000
Start-up inventory	$7,000
Other short-term assets	$1,000
Total short-term assets	$11,000
Long-term assets	$0
Total Assets	**$11,000**
Total Requirements	**$27,000**

Funding	
Investment	Amount
Luke Walsh	$10,900
Lisa Walsh	$2,900
Other	$0
Other	$0
Total Investment	**$13,800**

FIGURE 16-3. Start-up requirements (continued on next page)

Short-Term Liabilities	Amount
Unpaid expenses	$500
Short-term loans	$0
Interest-free short-term loans	$1,000
Total Short-Term Liabilities	$1,500
Long-Term Liabilities	$11,700
Total Liabilities	$13,200
Loss at Start-up	($16,000)
Total Capital	($2,200)
Total Capital and Liabilities	$11,000

FIGURE 16-3. Start-up requirements (continued)

2.3 Company Locations and Facilities

The company office is located in the owner's residence, 1455 Portland St., Bend, OR 97701. The office is about 1000 square feet and has ample space for the first three years of growth. Deliveries and shipments are serviced through the store located at 432 Smith Rock Drive, Redmond, OR 97756. The 5000-square-foot retail building is owned by The Boulder Stop and there is no excess storage capacity.

3.0 Products

Espresso is the big money maker for The Boulder Stop, with coffee peripherals coming in a close second. The rock-climbing gear is a long-term sales project that will rely on future catalog and word-of-mouth sales to achieve a positive ROI.

The Boulder Stop sells high-quality rock climbing gear to serious climbers. The gear is checked by knowledgeable employees who use and recommend equipment to customers and management. The gear is purchased from well-known manufacturers like Black Diamond, Boreal, and Petzl.

Straight espresso bean re-buys arrive on Mondays and Thursdays, ensuring the freshest beans possible. Modified re-buys begin on the first of each month. The owner will oversee all purchases, shipments, and deliveries.

3.1 Product Description

The Boulder Stop sells the entire raft of coffee drinks: lattes, mochas, cappuccino, espresso, and a delicious house blend. The coffee and espresso beans are freshly roasted by Espresso Harvest. Our team of two part-time high school students will create the beverages for customers. They will be trained in "The Art of Making the Proper Espresso Beverage" at Espresso Harvest, which hosts such classes once a month.

The Boulder Stop also sells carabiners, friends, nuts, ropes, webbing, shoes, and harnesses; our product mix is sufficient to satisfy even the most hard-core enthusiast. Below is a listing of some high-end products that we market:

- Black Diamond Camalot Camming Device—$50 to $100
- Wild Country Forged Friends with Sling—$35 to $65
- Hugh Banner HMS Locking Carabiner—$12 to $17
- The North Face Bouldering Sweatshirt, Men's—$85 to $105
- Mammut Flash Duodess 10.5 mm Dry Rope—$185 to $200
- Boreal Ace Rock Shoes—$150 to $170

All products are quality checked when they arrive and quality checked before the customer takes them home.

3.2 Competitive Comparison

The Boulder Stop has several advantages over its leading competitor.

1. Newer inventory and more modern interior fixtures.
2. Espresso drinks are made available to consumers while they shop, increasing marketing message impact. Our competitor offers the shopping experience that lacks the thrill of being able to sit down with friends, munch on a cookie, drink espresso and "talk shop."
3. The Boulder Stop is a fun, spacious store catering to both the climbing pros and the inexperienced. Our competitor, Rockage, is an exclusive pro shop that discourages some newcomers to the sport. Our positioning encourages those just getting started, a one-stop destination for equipment advice and purchasing opportunities, technique and safety instruction, and conversation with other enthusiasts.

3.3 Sourcing

Sourcing is critical for any enterprise, especially a retail operation. The Espresso Harvest will be our coffee vendors and will handle many in-store merchandising issues for their line of coffee products. Operational supplies for the coffee bar will be purchased from the regional supply wholesaler, which will handle special merchandising issues, such as point-of-sale materials. The sport and recreation inventory will be sourced directly from manufacturers like Black Diamond, Boreal, and Petzl.

3.4 Technology

We use off-the-shelf, PC-based software for accounting purposes, including AR/AP, inventory, purchasing, sales, and returns.

Our business plan is generated on an annual basis using Business Plan Pro from Palo Alto Software and reviewed quarterly for evaluation. Further functionality is provided by Palo Alto Software's companion package, Marketing Plan Pro, which allows us to make the most use of our marketing dollars by focusing our communications on target markets and enhancing our marketing knowledge.

We are in the process of implementing a Web site for The Boulder Stop. Online commerce is becoming an increasingly attractive option due to the relatively low cost of goods, the global reach of the medium, and the increasing security. Our business model could quite conceivably expand to include a form of Internet commerce in a variety of adventure equipment.

3.5 Future Products

Future expansion may allow for a horizontal increase of our product line by offering additional product categories: water sport gear, camping gear, and mountain biking accessories. We won't rule out the possibility of vertically integrating through our own line of climbing gear and/or espresso. We will also explore new services such as gear storage lockers, cellular phone rentals, and same-day guide services.

One dream the owner has is to develop an Internet environment within the store, not to remove people from those surrounding them, but to help them stay in touch with friends, family, and the latest information about rock climbing.

4.0 Market Analysis

Consumer expenditures for rock-climbing equipment rose to $4,000,000 in Central Oregon in 1997. We expect sales to increase steadily as Oregon's population grows and the rock-climbing industry becomes increasingly popular.

The Western Oregon presence of several large universities helps fuel our business, as does the status of Smith Rock as an international destination spot for rock-climbing enthusiasts. Individuals from as far away as Japan, Europe, South America, and Australia seek out Smith Rock as a beautiful and challenging sport- and rock-climbing destination. We count worldwide readers of such publications as *Rock & Ice* magazine and *Outdoor Adventure* among our target audience.

Our three main target markets are Weekend Warriors, Hard-Core Climbers, and the Curious. We predict that the number of Hard-Core Climbers will grow faster than the number of Weekend Warriors. Climbing is becoming more and more technical, an "insider's sport," and we believe this will fuel the growth of dedicated, highly sophisticated climbers.

This market analysis is somewhat conservative when compared with Oregon's predicted population growth of 2% per year and Bend's 5% average gains over the last five years.

4.1 Market Segmentation

- *The Weekend Warriors* purchase during weekends. When these climbers are on a rock wall, they want to look *cool*. They want to hang out with their friends at Smith Rock and enjoy a nice pre-climb or post-climb espresso drink or ice cream cone. Weekend Warriors pack special events with family members and friends. This market is our target for special events and climbing services such as tours and fun climbs.
- *Hard-Core Climbers* are very fickle about the gear they use. This segment is very brand loyal and provides

the company with powerful word-of-mouth marketing. They are highly sophisticated climbers who know the jargon and want to let everyone know they are serious about the sport and its image.

- *The Curious* want to stop in for a gander on their way to their campsites or hotel rooms. They may be into hiking Smith Rock State Park or just taking a driving tour: it doesn't matter. They may be travelers or locals, depending upon the season and the event.

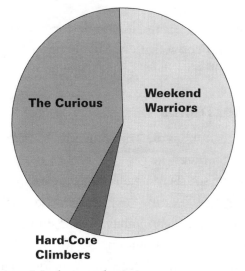

FIGURE 16-4. Market analysis

Potential Customers	Growth	1997	1998	1999	2000	2001	CAGR
Weekend Warriors	2%	40,000	40,600	41,209	41,827	42,454	1.50%
Hard-Core Climbers	2%	2,300	2,337	2,374	2,412	2,451	1.60%
The Curious	2%	30,000	30,600	31,212	31,836	32,473	2.00%
Total	1.71%	72,300	73,537	74,795	76,075	77,378	1.71%

FIGURE 16-5. Market analysis

4.2 Market Needs

There are two important underlying needs, and the combination of gear and coffee serves both. In many ways The Boulder Stop mimics the positioning of a ski lodge: selling crucial gear while providing a place for coffee, snacks, and talk.

1. There is a real need for a highly professional provider of climbing gear near the Smith Rock location. People forget to pack exactly what they need and things break.

2. There is also a practical need for coffee, a meeting place, and conversation. This is the activity focus of the location.

4.3 Market Trends

Trends are in our favor. There are three major trends at work in our market:

- Outdoor sports in general and rock climbing in particular are gaining exposure. The rock-climbing gyms in the Silicon Valley, Seattle, Eugene, and other locations are clear evidence of this trend.
- Central Oregon is becoming a major vacation destination and recreation spot.
- The gourmet coffee trend started in the Northwest and is spreading throughout the nation. A growing number of people look to their high-end coffee drinks as a way to enjoy a moment and as an integral part of any outing or activity.

4.4 Market Growth

- According to (the latest available studies), vacation spending in Oregon is growing more than 25% per year.

- Over the last five years, spending on climbing has been grown faster than spending on skiing or mountain biking, although from a much smaller base. According to [Omitted], the industry will experience 130% growth over the next three years.
- Coffee spending is up 15% this year, according to the [Omitted] annual report.

4.5 Industry Analysis

The rock-climbing industry is expanding faster than ever. Although climbing gear is priced at a premium, people buy it because it provides them with adventurous and, naturally, safer climbs.

Regarding the coffee shop market, high profit margins on coffee sales and low overhead costs lead to high profit margins in the espresso industry. Expansion of coffee and espresso retail outlets has increased exponentially in the last five years as large companies such as [Omitted] have increased their reach to the East Coast in cities such as Boston, New York, and Washington D.C.

4.6 Industry Participants

The rock-climbing gear industry is still fairly young. Climbing stores are generally small in size and community oriented. These stores seek to attract the most knowledgeable $6-$8/hour employees. There are some bigger players, such as [Omitted] that serve a larger, less targeted community with rock gear and gear for dozens of other outdoor sports. These national participants are consistent about their message and carry an impressive array of gear, but only the largest stores combine an espresso shop with the "Yuppie" shopping experience.

Participants in the espresso market are big-name retailers such as [Omitted] and [Omitted]. These retailers focus on the standardized model. Under this model, a buyer will get the same service and same beverage in New York as the one they will get in downtown Bend. This leads to a backlash of sorts, as local consumers move to industry participants that differentiate their companies from the national standardized model. The product becomes localized and the buyer recognizes the value of supporting a business that keeps its profits in the community that created the profit.

4.7 Competition and Buying Patterns

Climbers demand knowledgeable employees in a convenient location.

- **Comparison:** [Omitted] has placed its stores in urban industrial areas. [Omitted], a wholesaler, implements a similar strategy that draws the suburban dweller out of the house. This strategy keeps these customers isolated from the competition.
- **Products and services are the most important factors** when selling rock-climbing gear. Brand-name products sell well in stores that maintain a good selection, good location, and knowledgeable, friendly employees.
- **Espresso shops need to be fast, efficient, and friendly.** Fortunately, there are no espresso shops in close proximity to The Boulder Stop.

4.7.1 Main Competitors

Our nearest competitor is [Omitted]. Our next closest competitor is [Omitted], located in Redmond, seven miles from our store. Neither of these retailers offer espresso to their customers.

- [Omitted] sells limited gear (clothes); they do not promote or otherwise market their products extensively. They sell ice cream and carry more Gen X apparel than The Boulder Stop. In fact, their biggest strength may be that they may potentially become our ally. We see their products as complementary to ours: ice cream espresso. Their biggest weakness is limited store space.

- [Omitted] will be our toughest competitor, for they have already established themselves in the rock-climbing community. They have a very experienced and knowledgeable staff of expert climbers and are located on highway 97, two miles from Smith Rock. They carry 75%-80% of the same gear that we do.

5.0 Strategy and Implementation Summary

The Boulder Stop's main strategy is to develop The Boulder Stop experience as part of the rock-climbing activity. We don't intend to be just a store, but rather a rock-climbing cultural center for regulars and visitors to Smith Rock.

Underneath this strategy, our first tactic emphasizes the needs of the Hard-Core Climber. We assume that participation of the Hard-Core set will generate interest for others.

5.1 Value Proposition

The Boulder Stop gives Smith Rock visitors the highest-quality climbing gear, good coffee, and a place to meet, in a convenient locale.

5.2 Competitive Edge

Our location is a very important competitive edge. It will be difficult for our competitors to match our location. The other competitive edge in development is our reputation and involvement with the community. That is why we are developing a community of employees who are rock climbers, and our rock-climbing events, bulletin board, etc. This advantage is important to us because our prices are slightly higher than other cafes and other gear stores in Oregon.

5.3 Target Market Segment Strategy

We will focus on the highly discriminating Hard-Core Climber segment first, because these are the opinion leaders. Both the Weekend Warrior and the Curious will follow the Hard-Core Climbers. If we can attract and keep the Hard-Core Climbers, then they will attract others. To attract Hard-Core Climbers, we will carry all the best high-tech gear, know the jargon, use the latest technology, and become a "Futurist" product and services company.

We want to clearly differentiate the Weekend Warriors from the Hard-Core Climbers. Less competitive, or at least at a different competitive level, these climbers are usually at Smith Rock to hike or explore. They respect the Hard-Core Climbers, but don't want to be classified as having "rock on the brain." 20%-30% of these climbers will respond to family events by bringing their families; the other 70%-80% climb with friends and occasionally try to outdo each other. This market is highly susceptible to getting stuck in a coffee shop with friends; they will talk about their latest romance, conflicts with other friends, the future, or the fine espresso at The Boulder Stop. We will market the Weekend Warriors with a combination of amateur climbing events and family fun climbs.

5.4 Marketing Strategy

Our marketing strategy will focus on three segments. Those three segments are described in the following subtopics.

- The plan will benchmark our objectives for sales promotion, mass selling, and personal selling.
- We are focusing our marketing effort on the Weekend Warriors and the Hard-Core climbing community. We will implement a strategy that treats these customers as a community. This means our marketing resources will be centered around both sales promotions (events, displays) and personal sales (customer service, friendly atmosphere).
- The marketing budget will not exceed $5,000 per year.

Marketing promotions will be consistent with the Mission Statement.

5.4.1 Positioning Statement

For climbers who need a place to stop for gear and coffee near Smith Rock, The Boulder Stop offers high-quality climbing gear, gourmet espresso drinks, and a comfortable place to meet and talk. Unlike our competitors, our store is near the park and offers exactly what most climbers and tourists need.

5.4.2 Pricing Strategy

We will encourage impulse buying; therefore it is important that we maintain a flexible pricing strategy.

- Our pricing strategy will be based on competitive parity guidelines. We will not exceed competitors' prices by more than 10%, and if a customer sees a price elsewhere for less, we will give it to them for that price.
- Price says a lot about a product. The products that are innovative and not available elsewhere in the region will be marked up to meet the demand curve. We are not afraid of premium pricing a premium product.

- Espresso beverages will be priced slightly above the industry average. Although we will still be make money off our house coffee (not espresso), we consider this a "loss leader" product. Word-of-mouth advertising brings customers in for the house coffee, simply to make them aware of our additional products and services.

5.4.3 Sales Literature

The Boulder Stop will use advertising and sales programs to get the word out to customers.

- 2000 four-color brochures to be distributed throughout Bend and area facilities: outdoor clothing shops, hotels, ranger stations, chambers of commerce, tourism council offices, area eateries, and other tourist-frequented spots one month before the grand opening in May.
- Half-page newspaper advertisements in Oregon regional newspapers, advertising the following sales promotion: introductory rock-climbing classes, two days for $100 per person. Copy: magazine and newspaper advertisements.

5.4.4 Web Promotions

We will administer a Web site at www.boulder-stop.com. This Web site will present promotional material such as new marketing programs, product white papers, and contests. The site will allow for immediate purchase of gear online and will use a secure server to process transactions through CyberCash.

5.5 Advertising

Advertising costs are outsourced to [Omitted]. Most sales promotion and public relations work is handled in-house by Luke Walsh. Luke Walsh will write all product white papers and combine those with literature supplied by the manufacturer.

5.5.1 Seminars

Future seminars and climbing clinics will be handled either by the owner or by several certified and experienced tour and adventure professionals. We will use local contacts to research the availability of celebrity climbers to sponsor some of these clinics and events. We believe this tactic will build a grass-roots network of climbers that will help us to differentiate The Boulder Stop as a "hangout" for serious and curious climbers.

5.5.2 Promotion Strategy

The Boulder Stop will implement a strong sales promotion strategy. Advertising will be secondary.

- [Omitted] will be paid up to $4,000 to determine the needs of the surrounding population and how the company may best meet those needs with promotions, literature, and other marketing programs.
- Promotional campaigns will be partially outsourced to [Omitted].
- Sales promotions and public relation strategies will work together to inform customers of new products, to encourage an image of community involvement for The Boulder Stop, and to limit environmental impact.

5.5.3 Distribution Strategy

The customers will buy our products directly from the store, in the store. We will also generate sales through our Web site and its secure server and we will ship all ordered products from the store. All telephone orders will be taken at the store through either our single (800) line or the local number. Mail orders will be processed at the main office in Bend and shipped from the store. All debits and credits, order transactions, charge backs, and price discounts will be accounted for on the SBT Accounting system at the Bend office.

5.6 Sales Strategy

We will promote to the Weekend Warriors by hosting fun events like the "Fun Summer Climb '98." Our part-time sales clerks, also trained in the ways of promotional tactics, will call businesses within the Bend area and establish additional sponsors for these events. They will close the sale immediately if possible, enter the closure into the [omitted] software accounting system, and provide post sales follow-up.

For in-store sales, our strategy will be to maintain as much on-site point-of-purchase literature as is physically possible. Our part-timers will be responsible for informing customers of the products and creating the best fit between customer and product. Our salespeople will understand that selling is about filling a need, not pressuring the customer to buy. 70%-80% of returns will be sent back to the distributor or vendor.

5.6.1 Sales Forecast

The following table and chart give a rundown on forecasted sales. We expect sales to increase at a rate of 1%-2% per month for each product in the first few months. November through January will be slow months for The Boulder Stop. For February through March, we expect 1% monthly sales growth, becoming 2% growth as we reach the second summer. In 1999 and 2000, we expect solid 20%-25% sales growth as The Boulder Stop becomes well-known in Central Oregon. 1999 and 2000 costs will decrease 4%-7% due to lower agency and efficiency costs.

Note: For company purchases, the per-unit price of inventory purchases includes cost of shipping.

Sales	1998	1999	2000
Carabiners	$16,784	$20,141	$25,176
Ropes	$9,791	$11,749	$14,686
Books and magazines	$1,798	$2,158	$2,697
Cookies	$1,573	$1,888	$2,360
Espresso regulars	$57,695	$69,233	$86,542
Espresso shakes	$7,418	$8,901	$11,127
Gear rentals	$1,961	$2,353	$2,941
Other	$0	$0	$0
Total Sales	**$97,019**	**$116,423**	**$145,529**
Direct Cost of Sales			
Carabiners	$9,754	$8,779	$7,462
Ropes	$6,069	$5,462	$4,643
Books and magazines	$1,300	$1,170	$995
Cookies	$748	$673	$572
Espresso regulars	$30,148	$27,134	$23,064
Espresso shakes	$4,547	$4,092	$3,479
Gear rentals	$1,286	$1,158	$984
Other	$0	$0	$0
Subtotal Direct Cost of Sales	**$53,854**	**$48,468**	**$41,198**

FIGURE 16-6. Sales, projected by year

6.0 Management Summary

6.1. Management

Luke Walsh: Manager and founder

Luke spent four years selling shoes and apparel for Nordstrom, Inc. He graduated from the University of Oregon in 1997 with a degree in Business Management. Luke's success at Nordstrom, the University, and in building a network of close friends has hinged upon his "common sense" approach to solving ambiguous problems, his ability to identify strengths and weaknesses in the marketplace and exploit them, as well as his commitment to building strong relationships through trust.

6.2 Personnel Plan

The personnel plan is included in the following table. It shows the owner's salary (Other), followed by two part-time salaries for espresso servers/gear experts. Part-time employees will not be included in the profit-sharing program until they have worked with the company for 12 months.

Payroll	1998	1999	2000
Part-time employee #1	$4,700	$4,935	$5,182
Part-time employee #2	$4,700	$4,935	$5,182
Other	$0	$0	$0
Total Payroll	$9,400	$9,870	$10,364
Payroll Burden	$376	$395	$415
Total Payroll Expenditures	$9,776	$10,265	$10,779

FIGURE 16-7. Payroll, projected by year

7.0 Financial Plan

- Growth will be moderate, cash balance always positive.
- Marketing will remain at or below 15% of sales.
- The company will invest residual profits into company expansion and personnel.

7.1 Important Assumptions

We do not sell anything on credit. The personnel burden is very low because benefits are not paid to part-timers. And the short-term interest rate is extraordinarily low because of the owner's longstanding relationship with the USAA Credit Union.

	1998	1999	2000
Short-Term Interest Rate %	7.00%	7.00%	7.00%
Long-Term Interest Rate %	7.50%	7.50%	7.50%
Tax Rate %	30.00%	30.00%	30.00%
Expenses in Cash %	25.00%	25.00%	25.00%
Personnel Burden %	4.00%	4.00%	4.00%

FIGURE 16-8. Personnel burden, projected by year

7.2 Breakeven Analysis

For our breakeven analysis, we have chosen $3 to represent our average revenue per unit. Although revenue from ropes and other gear amounts to significantly more revenue per unit, such items skew the revenue curve toward less units sold. According to the analysis, we will break even at approximately $6,000 in monthly sales.

FIGURE 16-9. Breakeven analysis (breakeven point is where line intersects with $0)

7.3 Projected Profit and Loss

We predict advertising costs and consulting costs will go

up in the next three years. This will give The Boulder Stop a profit-to-sales ratio of nearly 31% by the year 2000. Normally, a start-up concern will operate with negative profits through the first two years. We will avoid that kind of operating loss by knowing our competitors, our target markets, industry direction, and the products we sell.

Note that we predict we will exceed our objective of 65% gross margin by the year 2000.

	1998	1999	2000
Sales	$97,019	$116,423	$145,529
Direct Cost of Sales	$53,854	$48,468	$41,198
Other	$0	$0	$0
Total Cost of Sales	$53,854	$48,468	$41,198
Gross Margin	$43,165	$67,955	$104,331
Gross Margin %	44.49%	58.37%	71.69%
Operating Expenses			
Advertising/Promotion	$3,740	$3,100	$3,500
Travel	$300	$0	$0
Miscellaneous	$0	$0	$0
Payroll Expense	$9,400	$9,870	$10,364
Payroll Burden	$376	$395	$415
Depreciation	$1,200	$1,236	$1,273
Leased Equipment	$0	$0	$0
Utilities	$1,569	$1,616	$1,665
Insurance	$780	$803	$828
Lease	$20,400	$21,012	$21,642
Other	$0	$0	$0
Contract/Consultants	$0	$0	$0
Total Operating Expenses	$37,765	$38,032	$39,686

FIGURE 16-10. Pro forma profit and loss statement (continued on next page)

Profit Before Interest and Taxes	$5,400	$29,922	$64,645
Interest Expense Short-Term	$0	$0	$0
Interest Expense Long-Term	$770	$572	$356
Taxes Incurred	$1,389	$8,805	$19,287
Extraordinary Items	$0	$0	$0
Net Profit	$3,241	$20,546	$45,003
Net Profit/Sales	3.34%	17.65%	30.92%

FIGURE 16-10. Pro forma profit and loss statement (continued)

7.4 Projected Cash Flow

We are positioning ourselves in the market as a medium-risk concern with steady cash flows. Accounts payable is paid at the end of each month while sales are in cash: this gives The Boulder Stop an excellent cash flow structure. Solid net working capital and intelligent marketing will secure a cash balance of $31,000 by January 1, 2000. Any amounts above $10,000 will be invested into semi-liquid stock portfolios to decrease the opportunity cost of cash held. The interest will show up as dividends in the cash flow table and will be updated quarterly (see Figure 16-11).

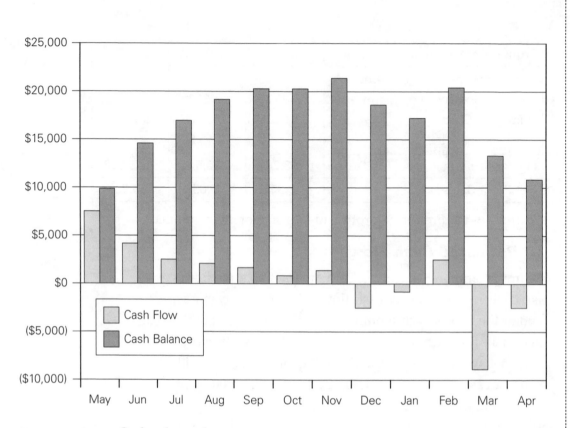

FIGURE 16-11. Cash, planned

	1998	1999	2000
Cash Received from Operations			
Cash Sales	$97,019	$116,423	$145,529
From Receivables	$0	$0	$0
Total Cash from Operations	$97,019	$116,423	$145,529
Additional Cash Received			
Extraordinary Items	$0	$0	$0
Sales Tax, VAT, HST/GST Received	$0	$0	$0
New Current Borrowing	$0	$0	$0
New Other Liabilities (Interest-Free)	$0	$0	$0
New Long-Term Liabilities	$0	$0	$0
Sales of Other Short-Term Assets	$0	$0	$0
Sales of Long-Term Assets	$0	$0	$0
Capital Input	$0	$0	$0
Subtotal Cash Received	$97,019	$116,423	$145,529
Expenditures from Operations			
Cash Spent on Costs and Expenses	$21,406	$22,380	$28,624
Wages, Salaries, Payroll Taxes, etc.	$9,776	$10,265	$10,778
Payment of Accounts Payable	$55,165	$43,729	($15,231)
Total Spent on Operations	$86,347	$76,374	$24,171
Additional Cash Spent			
Sales Tax, VAT, HST/GST Paid Out	$0	$0	$0
Principal Repayment of Current Borrowing	$0	$0	$0
Other Liabilities, Principal Repayment	$0	$0	$0
Long-Term Liabilities, Principal Repayment	$2,640	$2,880	$2,880
Purchase Other Short-Term Assets	$0	$0	$0
Purchase Long-Term Assets	$0	$0	$0
Dividends	$0	$0	$0
Adjustment for Assets Purchased on Credit	$0	$0	$0
Subtotal Cash Spent	$88,987	$79,254	$27,051
Net Cash Flow	$8,032	$37,169	$118,477
Cash Balance	$11,032	$48,202	$166,679

FIGURE 16-12. Pro forma cash flow

7.5 Projected Balance Sheet

All of our tables will be updated monthly to reflect past performance and future assumptions. Future assumptions will not be based on past performance but rather economic cycle activity, regional industry strength, and future cash flow possibilities. We expect solid growth in net worth beyond the year 2000.

ASSETS			
	1998	1999	2000
Short-Term Assets			
Cash	$11,032	$48,202	$166,679
Inventory	$3,697	($18,508)	($59,706)
Other Short-Term Assets	$1,000	$1,000	$1,000
Total Short-Term Assets	$15,729	$30,694	$107,973
Long-Term Assets			
Accumulated Depreciation	$1,200	$2,436	$3,709
Total Long-Term Assets	($1,200)	($2,436)	($3,709)
Total Assets	$14,529	$28,258	$104,264

LIABILITIES AND CAPITAL			
Short-Term Liabilities			
Accounts Payable	$9,552	$32,961	$134,063
Current Borrowing	$0	$0	$0
Other Short-Term Liabilities	$1,000	$1,000	$1,000
Total Short-Term Liabilities	$10,552	$33,961	$135,063
Long-Term Liabilities	$9,060	$6,180	$3,300
Total Liabilities	$19,612	$40,141	$138,363
Capital			
Paid-in Capital	$13,800	$13,800	$13,800
Retained Earnings	($16,000)	($12,759)	$7,787
Earnings	$3,241	$20,546	$45,003
Total Capital	$1,041	$21,587	$66,589
Total Liabilities and Capital	$20,653	$61,728	$204,953
Net Worth	($5,083)	($11,883)	($34,099)

FIGURE 16-13. Pro forma balance sheet

Appendix

BUSINESS PLAN CHECKLIST

THINGS YOUR PLAN SHOULD INCLUDE ◄

The points below are ones that you want to be sure your final plan covers. *If you missed one, you should go back and add it to the document.*

❑ 1. Give a short, clear description of exactly what your business is all about.

❑ 2. Explains why you are in business in terms of how:
   ❑ this opportunity is based on a customer need
   ❑ your management is suited to exploit this opportunity
   ❑ your approach to meet the opportunity is unique
   ❑ your offering is better

❑ 3. Clearly identify the key financial points about your business:
   ❑ sales forecasts
   ❑ gross margins
   ❑ earnings before interest, taxes, depreciation, and amortization
   ❑ how much money you need
   ❑ what money is already in the business and where it came from
   ❑ what the money will be used for
   ❑ what your offer is

❑ 4. Identify key characteristics of your target customers:

- ❏ how many
- ❏ how fast the market is growing
- ❏ how members of the target market spend money
- ❏ what they want

❏ 5. Show that the timing is right, in terms of:
  - ❏ market forces or conditions
  - ❏ your capabilities to deliver your product or service
  - ❏ your ability to attract resources

❏ 6. Demonstrate you can get the job done:
  - ❏ the management team
  - ❏ operations
  - ❏ marketing
  - ❏ market research

❏ 7. Explain why future growth exists:
  - ❏ market will need new products
  - ❏ margins will support growth
  - ❏ the company's vision is long term
  - ❏ timetables and objectives for growth

❏ 8. Show big payoff for investors:
  - ❏ an exit strategy
  - ❏ high growth conditions
  - ❏ good margins and low operating costs
  - ❏ modest financial requirements for growth

You will have an outstanding plan if someone reads it and can remember only these points. This is also the outline I use when making a presentation on a plan.

INDEX

Investment advice, 104–107
Investment needs, 53–59
Investment of excess funds, 181

J

Jawroski's Towing and Service GEL factor
    evaluation, 24–25, 42, 61–62

K

Key advantages, 119, 198, 224
Kinetix, 56
Kinko's GEL factor evaluation, 7–8
Kouba, Les C., 88, 90

L

Large accounts, focusing on, 15, 19
Latino consumers, health information for.
    See SanaSana business plan
Leverage ratio, 184
Levi Strauss, 55
Liquidity, quick ratio, 183
Location, 94
Long life
    as basic GEL factor, 4, 5
    evaluating investment required, 53–59
    evaluating profitability, 47–53
    major variables, 45
    sample evaluations, 59–63
Low-price products, 11

M

Management
    as business plan section, 166–170
    describing in executive summaries, 120
    financial experience, 170
    sample descriptions, 123–124, 173–175,
        196, 214, 243–244
Margins, evaluating, 47–48, 97
Market-based pricing, 100
Market changes, 51
Marketing
    alternative tactics, 55
    as business plan section, 156–160
    estimating expenses, 180
    promotional activities as key concern,
        38–40

sample descriptions, 160–165, 210–214,
    231–237
Marketing objectives, 158, 160, 210
Market niche, 18
Market research
    online services, 205–206
    sample descriptions, 142–145, 199
Market segments, 232–233
Market share, retaining, 55–56
Market size, describing, 119, 200–201, 203
Measurement
    business plans for, 112, 114
    of objectives, 160
Mission statements, 224
Monthly fees, 86

N

Natural fast food restaurant GEL factor
    evaluation, 23–24, 41–42, 60–61
Needs, as focus of marketing, 157
Net sales to inventory ratio, 184
Networking, 163
Network of contacts, 158
Newport, Calvin, 131–132

O

Objectives
    in executive summaries, 223
    marketing, 158, 160, 210
    measurability, 160
O'Naturals GEL factor evaluation, 23–24,
    41–42, 60–61
Ongoing product support, 50–53. *See also*
    Sales support
Online branding, 153
Online businesses. *See* Internet businesses
Operating earnings summaries, 216–217
Operations
    as business plan section, 166–173
    describing in business plans, 120
    sample descriptions, 215, 243–244
Opportunism, 36
Opportunities, describing, 122–123, 137–138
Outsourcing, 54–55, 168–169
Overhead, 48, 167–168